The Runner's Bible

The Peachtree Road Race in Atlanta, one of the nation's biggest road races. It's a 10K held every July 4 weekend, with upward of 50,000 participants.

The Runner's Bible

Marc Bloom

MAIN STREET BOOKS

DOUBLEDAY

NEW YORK LONDON TORONTO SYDNEY AUCKLAND

Other Books by Marc Bloom
CROSS COUNTRY RUNNING
THE MARATHON
OLYMPIC GOLD (with Frank Shorter)
KNOW YOUR GAME

A MAIN STREET BOOK
Published by Doubleday
a division of Bantam Doubleday Dell Publishing Group, Inc.
1540 Broadway, New York, New York 10036

MAIN STREET BOOKS, DOUBLEDAY, and the portrayal of
a building with a tree are trademarks of Doubleday, a division of
Bantam Doubleday Dell Publishing Group, Inc.

Drawings by Marian Pickman
Unless otherwise noted all photos courtesy of Marc Bloom

Library of Congress Cataloging-in-Publication Data

Bloom, Marc. 1947–
  The runner's bible
      Bibliography: p.129
  ISBN 0-385-18874-9
  1. Running.   2. Running races.
  3. Running races—United States—Directories.   I. Series.
GV1061.B56   1986
796.4'26 --   82-46075
                                CIP

18   17   16   15   14   13   12   11

Contents

1 Why Run?   1

Why people run. The benefits running provides. The different approaches to running success.

2 How to Start a Running Program   11

Preparing to take the first steps. Determining your goals. Your first month of running. A graduated training schedule.

3 How You'll Change As a Runner   26

Weight loss. Body consciousness. Muscular development. The perfect 10. Skin and bones. Daily habits. Friends. Enemies. Food. Sex. "Negative addiction."

4 How to Select the Right Gear and Equipment   35

What you need. Running-shoe considerations. The latest in running-shoe technology. Clothing. Running gadgets and high-tech equipment.

5 How to Develop
Strength and Flexibility   48

Flexibility through stretching. Do's and don'ts of
proper stretching. Developing a stretching program.
Strength through weight training. Types of weight training. Swimming.

6 Injuries, and What to Do
About Them   65

Why runners get injured. Injury prevention. When
injury strikes. Treatment of injury. Staying fit while
injured.

7 How to Cope the Elements and
Other Unpredictable Foes   82

The heat. Warm-weather precautions. The cold. Sur-
viving the winter. Hills. Running in the dark. Coping
with traffic. Dealing with dogs.

8 Eat and Run: A Skeptic's Dilemmia   99

Nutrition as an element of training. How running will
affect eating habits. Should you load up on carbohydrates? and other dietary issues.

9 How to Prepare for Racing   109

Planning for competition. How to find a suitable race.
Determining your goals. Before the race. Race strategy.

Race recovery. Evaluating your performance. Training
for future competition. Race pace chart.

10 How to Prepare for
    Your First Marathon   128
Making the commitment. Choosing a race. Prerace
preparation. Special nutritional considerations. How
to run a marathon. The wall. The finish. Recovery.
Your next marathon. Marathon training chart.

11 Special Running Considerations   145
Children. Senior citizens. Women.

12 A Program for the
    Advanced Runner   166
How the advanced runner should train.

Afterword   182

Appendix
    I   A Sampling of Leading American Road Races.   184

    II For Further Reading.   194

1

Why Run?

As millions of Americans and countless others across the world have found out, running is easy, fun and good for you. In fact, it's almost too good to be true. For the modest effort that you have to put into it to attain its essential benefits, running will provide so many of the necessities of health and fitness! The greatest irony of the fitness boom that has embraced our culture is the ease with which we can run and enjoy it. It was not all that long ago when we thought of running as a rather painful form of punishment best confined to gym class or boot camp. It was something you had to do, and you had to do it hard and fast, none of this jogging around. It was a complicated sort of physical ritual that had speed and aggressiveness as its underpinning, and who needed that?

But when people started to run in the late sixties and early seventies and we saw how simple it was to do at a leisurely pace and how great it felt, well, that was something of a miracle. Of course, that is why so many of us are running these days. Everybody loves a miracle, and the body in motion is indeed a miracle-working machine. It does everything.

WHY PEOPLE RUN

Running can help you lose weight. Running can build muscle tone. Running can improve your complexion. Running can strengthen your heart and make it work more efficiently. Running can increase your aerobic capacity and lower your blood pressure. Running can relax you,

1

Feelings of exhilaration, fulfillment, happiness and togetherness can come from running. And for women, in particular, a kind of freedom.

help you quit smoking, and reduce the risk of heart disease. Running can reduce depression and lift your spirits. Running can help you think and make you more creative. Running can make you more athletic and energetic and full of vitality. Running can improve your self-image and make you more self-confident.

In short, running can change your entire outlook on life and make a new person out of you.

We know this because fitness has become one of the most pervasive elements in American society, and we have taken to examining it quite carefully. The health professions in particular have sought to find out as scientifically as possible just what running and other forms of exercise can do for us, so we can go about improving our health and fitness systematically and for both short-term and long-term benefits. And every time a study is done the message is reaffirmed: running is good for you.

THE BENEFITS RUNNING PROVIDES

Tests are administered to determine how the body works under the influence of exercise, and what the effects might be. Physicians and physiologists test muscle, blood and oxygen; they test strength, stamina, endurance and exertion; they test mood and the mind. Runners pass with flying colors, thank you. To those of us who have been at it for some time, these findings come as no surprise. We have each been our own experiment. We know what running has done for us.

We also hear about it from others. For some reason, running converts like to talk about their newfound hobby, and so the neighbor, the postman and the fellow worker in the office across the hall have stories to tell, notes to compare, providing further anecdotal support for running as the cornerstone of the fitness movement. A friend of mine who at one time ridiculed running finally took to it and after his first race he spoke of little else. Another friend, a basketball coach who, despite being a natural athlete, never showed much talent for running in his youth, got serious about running and became a marathoner. A Vietnam veteran and heavy smoker started jogging one day to release tension, and now he never misses a day. He never smokes, either. A woman who never had an interest in sports or exercise tried running to lose weight, fell in love with running and is now far more concerned with counting miles than calories.

Running is the "drug" of the nineties. Running clearly has addictive qualities—there are tests for that, too—and many of those who take it up find it hard to put down. That may not always be so good, because there comes a point when you can run to excess, and then you defeat the purpose of running in the first place. Running to excess is a form of "anti-fitness"; it starts to reverse the progress you've made toward better health and a better life.

The wonders of running may be hard to swallow for those who have never tried it, or those who have tried running but didn't give it enough of a chance, or those who rushed into it without sufficient briefing as to how to go about it. It is natural for these people to be incredulous. Or for them to conclude, "Running is not for me." Running, surely, is not for everyone. But I believe it is for most people. What many of the disbelievers probably do not realize is that the approach to running can differ, depending on the individual. The amount and intensity of running will vary greatly from one person to the next, as will the emphasis given running in one's overall fitness program. It helps, ultimately, if you "like" running. But even that is not mandatory. One can run only a little and participate in other, more game-like or team-oriented, activities as well and feel good about running's benefits without longing for the daily fix as others do.

And to those already fixed on running, I wonder how many of you are getting the most out of it. I wonder how many of you are realizing your athletic potential, if that is your aim. I wonder how many of you are experiencing difficulty with your running because of misinformation about it, or because you're unaware of the recent developments in exercise physiology and sports medicine that can enhance and bolster your fitness program.

Now, in the mid-nineties, we are entering the second generation of

This shot of Gayle Barron, a former winner of the Boston Marathon, represents the feeling of fitness, vitality and happiness derived through running. *(Bill Grimes)*

running. The investigation of running continues, and we are starting to challenge some of the assumptions we made when running first became popular. Also we, as experienced runners, are changing. We don't necessarily want the same things from running that we craved at the outset. And, as well, the opportunities are broadening. Running, for a lot of people, is no longer the sole physical activity, but a part of a more well-rounded program for total body conditioning.

Our purpose here, then, is twofold: to introduce running to those neophytes just starting to become fitness-minded, and to help the experienced runner derive greater benefit from the sport he or she already knows a good deal about.

DIFFERENT APPROACHES TO RUNNING

In running, there are three distinct levels of commitment. 1. You can run for basic health and fitness. 2. You can run, or "train," for competition of medium distance. 3. You can train for competition of long distance, that is, the marathon. Though there are shades of commitment within each level, most runners can be categorized in one of the three groups; and it should be emphasized that I'm not referring to ability or performance, but *commitment*. It is from that point that everything else develops. In each category, a range of ability can be found.

Running for Basic Health and Fitness

Most runners start out with this goal in mind. The achievement of a state of fitness can be an end in itself, or a way station that leads to more ambitious goals. The more ambitious approach is not to be considered "better" than the modest one. It depends on what you want out of running. The term *better* should be used in another context: from running, you should hope to better yourself, and you can do that even with a minimal program of exercise. This exercise, moreover, will serve you best if you can develop a fit-and-healthy state of mind and incorporate the habits of fitness into your lifestyle. That means, essentially, no smoking, sensible eating, modest alcohol intake and an emotionally comfortable approach to things, including exercise.

The vast majority of America's 30 million runners exercise for health and fitness and not for racing performance. They run for weight control, to be in shape for other sports, to meet people in a social setting, to relax after a hard day's work, for rehabilitation after illness or injury, and because they simply enjoy it.

A number of programs have been advanced by exercise physiologists and doctors regarding the scope of running for minimum fitness levels. The consensus is that if you run four times a week for thirty minutes, each time at a pace that brings your heart rate to 75 percent of its maximum capacity, you'll be doing just fine. In due time, if you keep it up, you'll start to lose weight, firm up, improve your oxygen intake, lower your pulse, strengthen your heart and eliminate disease-causing elements from your system.

Training for Medium-Distance Competition

Training is different from just plain running. It's the difference between tossing the football around every other day and trying out for the team. Running for fitness is casual, somewhat informal, and though the objectives are important—even critical—once you attain the desired results there is little urgency to the program. You run a few miles here and a few miles there, and you've got it.

In training, you enter an entirely new dimension, and that is because you need to develop your system so that it can function in competition—in a race—and ultimately at a certain level of performance. In that sense you are no different from the champions, except that the champions can run faster and have more time to train, because running is their "work"—their source of income. The race makes the same demands upon all of us, and we must train to be able to meet those demands.

With road racing firmly implanted in our national sports system, there are more competitive opportunities than ever before for the recreational runner. The most common racing distance is 10,000 meters (10 kilometers), or 6.2 miles. The next-most-common distance is 5 miles. This is what we used to call long-distance, but now, with our perceptions of distance and exertion having undergone a metamorphosis, we consider it medium-distance. Events that are longer, the 10-milers and half-marathons and marathons and beyond, are the long-distance races.

People who develop an interest in competition are at first usually bitten by the challenge of merely completing the distance. Even if they have run five or six miles in their day-to-day running, that is not the same thing as doing it in a racing environment, with hundreds or thousands of runners all around and the wonderful feeling of accomplishment and recognition that is a part of such an experience.

One can be running for basic fitness for a period of time, say for as little as three months, and possibly be fit enough to plan to tackle a race simply for the purpose of finishing it. Frequently, the largest segment of the racing population is the group that is just getting into shape and looking for a new challenge. Racing is a marvelous challenge, because

The running boom has also grown worldwide. This shot shows Maricica Puica of Romania and Wendy Sly of Great Britain.

everything about it is so logical. Before you can expect to reach certain goals in competition, you need to train according to a certain formula, and the methods can be laid out very precisely as part of a step-by-step plan. (And we'll get to that soon enough.)

A most profound demand of running comes when you reach the point when you can comfortably complete the racing distance and then wish to embark on a training program designed to improve your time—that is, enable you to run faster for the given distance. This is when you start to wonder how much your body can take and how much time you can devote to running to bring about the desired training effect. Great care is needed to make sure you won't do too much too soon. Most runners try a little too hard, which is why there is a growing need for doctors who specialize in sports medicine and the treatment of injury.

Training for Long-Distance Competition

Training philosophy is the same for long-distance as for medium-distance: get the body (and mind) ready to meet the demands of the event. The long-distance event to which many runners aspire is the marathon, the famous 26-mile 385-yard race that has become enormously popular and is considered the ultimate challenge of conventional running.

I am not entirely happy about the popularity of the marathon. Too many runners feel an obligation to run it. It is as though they cannot feel they are serious runners until they have met the challenge of the marathon. Indeed I have come across people who, after a month or so of fitness jogging, want to know what they have to do to train for a marathon.

Marathon running requires an enormous commitment, much more so than the medium distances, in terms of time and effort.

The training equation for the marathon requires a great deal of time spent running, especially if your goal becomes to do it in a respectable time for your age and experience. It is not uncommon to find marathon runners who have had to change much about their lives to accommodate the training needed to enable them to run 26.2 miles successfully.

This doesn't mean the marathon is not worth trying for. It may well be. It has a lot to offer almost anyone in the way of accomplishment, recognition, self-respect and athletic conditioning. It is also potentially hazardous. The more ambitious a training program, the greater the chances of injury; the more involved you are in running in general, the

The running pop-
ulation is hardly
homogeneous; it's
made up of all
sorts of men and
women with a
variety of goals.

greater the chance it will conflict with other aspects of your life such as work and family obligations.

It is important to keep the marathon in perspective. Running does not have to be the controlling element in your life, but if you become a marathon runner it probably will be, for a while. Some people want that, others don't.

It's easy to get hooked on the marathon because of the glamorous role it's taken on in the sport. The major marathons make headlines in newspapers and magazines and are now covered on television. Their six-figure budgets are supported by corporate sponsors. The big stars are household names: Bill Rodgers, Frank Shorter, Alberto Salazar, Grete Waitz, Joan Benoit. Marathons inspire great hoopla and some-times even controversy, and the great cities of our nation—New York, Boston, Chicago, Los Angeles and the rest—open up to them with an outpouring of municipal support. Today a major marathon is one huge running feast. Even people who don't know a thing about running have a vague idea of what a marathon is all about.

So it's natural for the developing runner who is amazed at his or her progress to sit back on a Sunday afternoon after a nice run, sip a cold beer, and think about how nice it would be to run a marathon someday. If that runner is you, just be prepared to make the commitment.

Whether you choose to run for health and fitness, or train for competition, you'll find that the process of getting in shape is exciting and rewarding for its own sake.

2

How to Start a Running Program

The most important factor in the ultimate success of a running program is the extent to which you allow for gradual development. A
sedentary person who decides to run five miles the first day is asking for
trouble. So might the individual whose exercise has come from bowling, basketball or tennis. Running is different, even slow running,
because, unlike most other sports, it is continuous. It places different
strains on the muscles, lungs and heart. These are good strains, because
they will produce physical fitness; however, a body that has been suffering from disuse cannot be expected to take on very much at the outset.
And running is physical work.

PREPARING TO TAKE THE FIRST STEPS

The initial responsibility in the developmental process is to make sure
that you are healthy enough—or not too unhealthy —to take on the stress
of a running program. Certain people, because of age, heredity or lifestyle,
are afflicted with conditions (perhaps even unknown to them) that would
become dangerous to their health and even fatal if under the influence of
something like running. Others have conditions, obesity for one, that can
improve with exercise such as running but require a particularly prudent
and perhaps medically supervised approach to the sport.

The first step, then, for some people is to undergo a stress test. You
might consider this an "exercise tolerance" test. The main part of it
involves walking or running on a treadmill so that work-load tolerance
can be determined. The typical family doctor does not have the equip-

ment or the familiarity with fitness to administer such a test, and so you must look for it at a college, YMCA, private fitness center or the like. Most doctors recommend that "high-risk" individuals take such a test before embarking on a running program. For example, someone who is over forty, out of shape, and a smoker and has heart disease in his family would be wise to be tested first.

Dr. Kenneth Cooper, the world-famous aerobics evangelist, reports, "... in our ten years of testing more than 43,000 people on treadmills at the Aerobics Center, we found 126 patients who subsequently had a major coronary attack or had serious problems which led to surgery." Though the percentage of the seriously ill was tiny, those 126 cases were studied, and Cooper's staff discovered the following: some had high blood sugar; one out of four had an abnormal resting EKG; one third smoked at the time of their visit; many showed a relatively high level of cholesterol; almost three quarters showed abnormal stress EKG's; a majority of the people who died were overweight (i.e., the men had more than 19 percent body fat, the women had more than 22 percent). Cooper, in his book, *The Aerobics Program for Total Well-Being,* claims that the most reliable predictor of impending heart ailment is the time it takes one to walk to exhaustion on the treadmill. Explains Cooper: "We've established a minimum standard for the average middle-aged patient of walking 15 minutes or longer on the treadmill, which is roughly equivalent to running two miles in 20 minutes... Unless you have reached this minimum fitness level, it doesn't appear that you have any protection from coronary disease." Fully 80 percent of the 126 cases were unable to walk 15 minutes on the treadmill.

When you are ready to begin running, there is little to deal with. Since running is not a skill sport in the sense that tennis is, there are no techniques to learn before you can actually "play." In running, you simply... run. Or, at your beginner's pace, you'd probably call it jogging. You'll notice the word *jogging* missing from most of this book. I don't like the sound of it. Whether you jog or run is a question of semantics more than commitment or ability. Generally slow running is considered jogging, but I think you're better off considering yourself a runner from the start. After a while you'll know what I mean.

There are a few things to be aware of before you take your very first running steps. You have to have the right gear, you have to know about

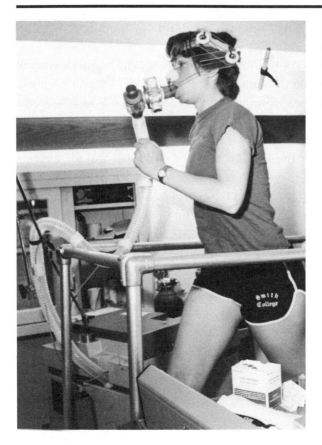

New runners are
sometimes given
exercise tests to
determine their
level of fitness.

warming up and warming down, and you have to have an open mind about what you're setting out to do.

Gear includes two things: clothing and shoes. Your clothing must match the weather and your shoes must match your feet. Obvious, you say. From some of the novice runners I've seen, apparently it's not so obvious. Runners are becoming a little too brand-conscious, thinking they've got to acquire a certain company's clothing or shoes. They don't realize there is a wide variety of high-quality goods on the market today, and that function, fit and comfort are the most critical in apparel and shoes for pleasurable and productive running. Styling is much improved too, so you can look good and feel good at the same time—with or without "designer labels." I'll discuss clothing in detail in Chapter 4, but for now make sure you've given some thought to your gear and that you have a pair of supportive and durable training shoes with which to start running.

As you progress in your running, the warm-up and warm-down will become more important, because your pace and mileage will advance. Even at the outset, a warm-up can help to trigger the body's systems for exercise, and conversely, a warm-down at the end of the session will properly return the body to its resting state. This is generally done in two ways: with stretching exercises and (if you'll pardon the expression) a short period of jogging. After a short while in your running program your pace will have reached the level where additional jogging will be unnecessary, so what you need to do then is a little light stretching before and after the run. You have to approach stretching just as you approach running, with care and caution. Much has been written

It's important to do stretching exercises as part of a warm-up. This happens to be U.S. mile record holder Steve Scott. *(Steven Sutton/ DUOMO)*

More on warming up, this time before a race.

about stretching, pro and con, but my advice regarding stretching as you start your running program is, Less is better. From what you find in Chapter 5, select three or four simple exercises that you feel comfortable with, and do them before and after running; you can always add more if you need to. The most important part of the body to untighten is probably the backs of the legs—the calves and hamstring muscles—so make sure you select a stretching exercise that will help to relax these muscles.

You need an open mind about running, because the actual experience may feel different from what you expect. You may find you get more, or less, out of it than you anticipate. You may find you're good at it, or that it's a real chore. You may feel awkward doing it, or even embarrassed. You may find your running friends giving you a lot of conflicting advice. You must proceed with the idea that you are your own personal experiment, and that you will judge the merits of running based on what it feels like to you. Don't go in with unrealistic expectations. The miracle-working benefits of running do not take effect overnight, or even in the course of a few days or a week.

DETERMINING YOUR GOALS

At the outset, you should have but one goal in mind: to run regularly for one month. At the end of that time, take stock of what you're doing and decide what sort of running you should do from that point on.

The First Day

You're wearing the proper attire, including good shoes. You've done some light stretching. You're committed to seeing this through for at least a month. You're ready to run.

On the first day, try fifteen minutes of movement. I say movement because it's all right to walk as well as run. But don't allow yourself to walk more than you run in those fifteen minutes, and of course try to run for the whole time. But you can intersperse some walking with the running if you feel you need to. There's nothing wrong with that. Soon enough you won't need to walk.

If you run for the whole time, the distance covered will probably be between one and one-and-a-half miles. Don't be any more ambitious the first day. Try not to tackle any hills in the beginning. Any flat area is good, and I recommend ordinary roads instead of a track, because it's not a good habit to rely on a track. A track does have its advantages (no cars, distance easily computed, etc.), but it will limit your enjoyment of running as you develop, and with other runners likely to be out on the track at the same time, it's too easy to get "sucked" into a pace or distance that you're not yet ready for.

Don't worry about how you're running. Just run in as natural a way as possible, as long as your body is fairly erect (possibly with a bit of a foreward lean), your head up (not tilted) and your arms about waist-high and moving more in a front-and-back motion than a side-to-side motion. These are not rules, just things to be aware of. Ultimately, your

A point about running form: Joan Samuelson's torso is over her center of gravity, she's getting some knee lift, her head is straight, and her stride is open. *(Steven Sutton/ DUOMO)*

style will go through some changes and whatever form you adopt probably will be natural for your body type and particular mechanics of movement.

If you feel great the first day, like a million dollars, you're an exception. Most newcomers feel a little strained and sluggish and may complain of leg-muscle stiffness. It's normal. Even if you've run your fifteen minutes at a very relaxed, "conversational" pace, as you certainly should have, your breathing probably will have felt a little forced and your muscles a little tight. But then, that's what getting in shape is all about. You probably feel not much different from major-league ballplay-

It's a good idea for new runners to do some running on soft surfaces (such as the grassy fields found in parks), to reduce the shock to their legs. *(Bill Grimes)*

ers on their first day of spring training after a winter's layoff. And no matter how out of sorts you may feel physically, I'd bet you'll feel pretty good emotionally because you've accomplished something. You've run for fifteen minutes, and you're ready to try it again.

YOUR FIRST MONTH OF RUNNING

Here is a running schedule for your first month. In this schedule, I use time running instead of mileage. It is meant as a guide. It may be too ambitious for some runners, and not ample enough for others. It is

Running on dirt trails is another way for beginners to reduce shock to the legs.

designed to achieve a level of fitness that will have you running for thirty minutes by the end of a month.

It is essential, in the first month, that you try for consistency. A training effect can take place only if exercise is done on a regular basis, and even then, as I've said, it takes time. Also, for your emotional well-being, you'll feel better about any conditioning program that you adhere to, even if results come slowly.

All training improvement is based on effort and recovery, and that's why I advise essentially alternating days running with days off at the outset. Your system will need to recover in order to be able to make an effec-

tive effort the next time out and not eventually become "overloaded." Even top runners adhere to this hard/easy principle. Someone like Bill Rodgers might run hard four days a week and "easy" the other days.

Many things will occur to you as you run from day to day that you hadn't thought of initially. You'll feel terrible one day and wonder if it's worth it. (It is.) You'll feel terrific another day and wonder if you can run an extra mile. (Don't.) You'll see a little kid or senior citizen running along at a brisk pace and wonder why that can't be your pace too. (In due time it will.) Your leg muscles may feel stiff in the mornings and you'll wonder what you can do about that. (Be patient; better fitness will take care of that.) You may develop localized areas of tenderness in muscles or joints that are discomforting and wonder what to do about that. (Most such minor irritations are helped with applications of ice—see Chapter 6, injuries.) You may get tired at an earlier hour and wonder if you're ill. (No, it's a good fatigue from the running and you'll sleep better.) You'll get occasional "stitches" in the side and wonder if it's from something you ate. (It may well be, and you'll have to learn how to adjust your meals and eating habits with your running. Most people have to leave at least two hours between a meal and a workout.) If it's hot you'll feel less hungry and more thirsty and wonder if that's normal. (It is, and it's important to take in water and other fluids in ample amounts in warm-weather running.) You'll hear about road races and "fun runs" and wonder when you'll be able to try one. (Be patient— your turn will come.)

If for any reason, by the end of a month, you are unable to run comfortably for thirty minutes without stopping, it does not mean you have failed, or even that you are less predisposed to successful running than the next person. We all react differently to running, especially in the beginning, and even some of the champions you see winning races today had difficulty starting out. Take as long as you need to reach the

There isn't only one "correct" way to run. Allison Roe, on the right, has a long stride and more of an "open" style. Jan Merrill has a shorter stride, but her style is efficient for her. *(Gale Constable/DUOMO)*

	Day 1	Day 2	Day 3	Day 4	Day 5	Day 6	Day 7
Week 1	15 min	____	15 min	____	10 min	____	15 min
Week 2	20 min	____	20 min	____	10 min	____	20 min
Week 3	25 min	____	25 min	____	15 min	____	25 min
Week 4	25 min	____	25 min	____	20 min	____	30 min

thirty-minute goal, and when you do, give yourself a pat on the back, because that's something to be proud of. It means you're able to run three miles.

Then take stock of what you've done, how much you enjoy running and how it fits in with your lifestyle and other exercise you may do. If you feel thirty minutes four times a week is enough for you, fine, continue with that. It will provide you, over time, with enough exercise for your system, the heart in particular, to maintain a healthy state. This is especially true if you are also involved in other sports, such as swimming, biking or weight lifting.

A GRADUATED TRAINING SCHEDULE

Running twelve miles a week is a fairly significant load, however, and you'll benefit by knowing more of what is discussed in the rest of this book, as far as injuries and equipment and nutrition are concerned.

Incidentally, as your planning changes from time spent running to specific mileage, you'll need to be more aware of distance covered. A good sense of pace will help you determine your mileage, but if that's not good enough for you, simply take your car over your running routes to confirm your distances.

If you're hooked after the first month and wish to further develop your running, continue it as shown in the chart.

The goal, as you can see, is to bring you to twenty-five miles a week by the end of the third month. As in the program at the outset, this may be easy for some people and difficult to others. If you need additional weeks to enable you to run five miles a day for five days in a given week, take it. It is better to take it more slowly than to fight through any sort of discomfort just to fulfill mileage quotas. I must emphasize that these monthly schedules are meant only as a guide to show the kind of approach taken in a beginner's running program.

THE SECOND MONTH	Day 1	Day 2	Day 3	Day 4	Day 5	Day 6	Day 7
Week 1	3*	___	3	___	3	___	3
Week 2	3	___	4	___	3	___	4
Week 3	4	___	4	___	4	___	4
Week 4	4	___	4	___	4	2	4
THE THIRD MONTH	Day 1	Day 2	Day 3	Day 4	Day 5	Day 6	Day 7
Week 1	4	___	4	___	4	2	5
Week 2	4	___	4	___	5	2	5
Week 3	5	___	4	___	5	3	5
Week 4	5	___	5	___	5	5	5

* Figures represent miles

There is an addictive quality to running, and no one better exemplifies that than Ron Hill of Great Britain, who has run every single day since October 1964, the world's longest running streak. He was an Olympic marathoner in 1972 and is a past winner of the Boston Marathon.

There is no age limitation to a successful running program.

Bear in mind several other factors as you run in the second and third months. Don't let foul weather prevent you from running, unless hazardous conditions exist, such as ice and snow, and in the summer, extreme heat and humidity. Use common sense and trial and error as a guide. Your running pace must continue to be that which is comfortable, which may be anywhere from eight to twelve minutes a mile. Though most of your running should be done on reasonably flat terrain, you can do some running on hills (see Chapter 7), but make sure you never cut loose with abandon and run at a reckless speed on the downhills. If you do, you'll pay for it. On the subject of speed, I have not yet included any sort of "speed work"; that will come later on. For now, your running is to be leisurely, to acquire the fitness to develop a foundation of conditioning on which to build for future performance. You'll find perhaps that you're starting to lose weight. Indeed, weight loss may have been an important running goal for you. Be careful to monitor your weight loss, and also not to become fanatical about it. Because of your exercise you will likely lose weight and tone your muscles, especially if you also reduce your food intake. A sensible diet along with regular exercise is the best health plan for weight control (see Chapter 8).

After three months of consistent running, reaching a point where you can run twenty-five miles a week, you can consider yourself a confirmed runner. Twenty-five miles a week is fairly substantial, and so at this point you should simply try to maintain that workload. Don't increase your mileage. Continue to hit twenty-five a week for another month. Don't run more than five days a week, and don't vary much from your maximum of five miles at one time. What you will find in the course of the fourth month is that your pace will improve. You may not even be conscious of it, but I can almost guarantee that toward the end of the month there will be more of a spring in your stride.

With four months and about 275 miles under your belt, you will have graduated from the beginner's program and will be ready to consider competition, if that is your goal. Competition, as I've stated, brings with it a new way of looking at yourself and your sport. The next six chapters cover various aspects of running and fitness that will be important to your over-all running program. We pick up with advanced training for competition in Chapter 9.

3

How You'll Change
As a Runner

The world is divided into two kinds of people: runners and nonrunners. Runners live a certain way, and nonrunners, by and large, live a different way. This has little to do with age, income, religion or politics. Runners are different because of their running. Though running, as we have seen, is a rather simple exercise, it can change people in profound ways. These changes are associated with the lifestyle that is taken on to facilitate a serious running program, and also with the effects running has on the body and mind. Let's take a look at a number of common transformations, so you can be ready for them when they come.

WEIGHT LOSS

The most obvious change is that you will look different, perhaps to others even more so than to yourself. If you are overweight, you'll lose some weight; if you are not overweight, you'll still "tighten up." Friends and family will notice. Even a few pounds will matter, for the better. But, more commonly, new runners find that, in several months, they've lost ten or twenty pounds or more, because they came into running in a sedentary and out-of-shape state. To be running and (finally) trim triggers off a whole range of physical and emotional changes.

BODY CONSCIOUSNESS

While, before, your body may have embarrassed you, running will make you proud of it, and you will become more sensitive to its look, feel and state. That is, you will become more conscious of its working parts (and not only during exercise) and how those parts function interdependently in the exercise process. You'll become a good judge of your personal level of fitness, and you'll acquire an ability to better weigh the little aches and pains that running can produce as well.

MUSCULAR DEVELOPMENT

Though you will become thin (or thinner), you will also develop muscular strength and definition. Only muscle that is worked can develop. In running, the lower body is stressed far more than the upper body, and so the muscles you develop will be in the legs, as opposed to the arms, chest and shoulders. And it will be in the backs of the legs (the calf and hamstring muscles) more than the front (shin and quadriceps), because most distance runners strike the ground with their heels, driving force up through the posterior. (Sprinters, on the other hand, run on their toes and develop the fronts of their legs.) This development is entirely desirable and a good sign that you're gaining fitness. Sometimes women fear that, because of leg muscles, they will start to look "masculine." Nonsense. First of all, because women anatomically have less muscle than men, there is less to develop, and that's why you don't see many women with noticeably defined muscle. But those that do acquire it are proud of it, and rightly so.

THE PERFECT 10

As long ago as March 1980, a cover story appeared in *The Runner* magazine titled "Body Images." In it, writer Laurie Stone analyzed our changing views of attractiveness and sexuality as they related to the running and fitness movement. The subtitle on the cover was "Leaner Men, Stronger Women," and the article explained how running, among other things, had changed our attitudes toward what our bodies should look like, and how our bodies reflected a changing social sensibility. In other words, being lithe and "running-thin" was becoming the ideal for men, in contrast to the old ideal of the macho tough guy; and becoming strong and "muscular" through running was the ideal for women, in contrast to the big-busted curvaceous and helpless Marilyn Monroe ideals of previous times.

Mary Slaney: Women who run a lot should not fear that they'll develop unwanted muscle. Slaney has an excellent muscle tone, not muscle bulk.

If your running reaches the marathon training level and you're putting in upward of fifty miles a week, you could, depending on your bone structure, develop the sort of gaunt, sunken-cheeks look that will cause your mother to wonder if you're getting enough to eat. To other runners you will look enviably good. To nonrunners you will look "bad." For most marathoners this is a temporary state anyway, because after the marathon, depression and pigging out will restore a little fat to your cells.

DAILY HABITS

For everybody there is a good time of day to run and a bad time, and when you determine your good time, everything else in your life that is at all flexible will tend to revolve around your workout. This is more significant than it may seem at first thought. Since when you run also determines when you eat, when you shower, when you work (in some cases), when you move your bowels, when you make love, when you spend time with the kids, and much else, the run will establish your pattern of activity throughout the day—except for your basic work hours, which for most people are fairly stable. This is just the sort of thing that nonrunners cannot understand but every runner knows is true.

It is true whether you run before work, at 6 A.M., or after work, at 6 P.M., or during your lunch hour, or in the morning and the evening because you've advanced to double workouts. Since every runner also knows it is imperative to be consistent, your life will take on a distinct pattern and you will be habitual about much that you do, simply because you run every day at a specified time.

My household is a case in point. My wife enjoys running early in the morning, and fortunately I don't. She'll get up at six and run from six-thirty to seven-thirty and feel great. I can barely walk at that hour, and while she's out running I'll give our two daughters breakfast and help get the older one ready for school. By eight I'm out the door for my long commute into the city. Frankly, I'd prefer to leave for work a little earlier, but I can't, because my wife needs to run and to ask her to get up even earlier than six would be unfair.

With a shower available at the office, I run at lunchtime, and since that sometimes stretches the lunch hour, I'll work into the evening and frequently come home later than I (and my family) would prefer. But I've got to run. So there are compromises left and right. Even my

Note the strength of Jeanette Bolden, a leading sprinter. Despite suffering from asthma, she has been able to run very well.

twelve-year-old makes them. She's hungry when she comes home from school. But she runs during the week and postpones her afternoon snack until she's through running.

A runner's habits manifest themselves in many ways, some of them seemingly anti-social. To be fully rested for the traditional Sunday-morning long run, the runner is not likely to be found among the late revelers on a Saturday night. If only one spouse or mate runs and the other enjoys a few drinks and a lot of laughs on a Saturday night, there is potential conflict. Statistics have shown that in such a relationship, "the loneliness of the long-distance marriage" can sometimes lead to divorce.

FRIENDS

Men go bowling, play poker and go out drinking. Women... well, I'm not quite sure what it is that women have traditionally done together, but whatever it is, women runners probably don't do much of it. Because of the time and effort required in running, and also because of the expanded body consciousness, runners sometimes start to drift away from people who are not runners. They start to have less and less in common with nonrunners and live a more controlled and less self-abusive life.

ENEMIES

You will start to hate smokers. Some of these people will be your friends. People who smoke do not run, and they rarely exercise. They're frequently overweight.

You'll start to avoid them and their kind.

You may eventually develop an anti-nonrunner snobbishness, but this attitude is to be avoided, because it's no better than the antirunner attitude you'll find in some other people. At its worst, the anti-nonrunner holds that people who run are "better" than people who don't. This, of course, is foolish thinking. It is usually espoused by runners who feel that an evening spent talking about running constitutes a wonderful time.

FOOD

Most runners find that when they start running, the exercise suppresses their appetite, and that's one of the reasons weight loss usually comes about. However, in due time, as you become more comfortable with running and you do more of it, your appetite will probably be what it's always been, if not more so. Because of the exercise, you'll be able to eat more and not gain weight. Everyone in the Western world dreams of being able to eat to his or her heart's content and not gain weight, and so you will be the envy of nonrunners, who will sneer with disgust at how much you can eat and still look trim.

Your pattern of eating will change as a runner, and your diet may also change as your body craves different foods and you become more aware of the "fuel" your body needs to perform well. Before you took up running, you probably slept late on the weekend, ate a big breakfast, ate lunch, snacked while you watched sports or whatever on TV, and then ate a substantial dinner. You probably took in too much protein and fat in relation to carbohydrates. As a runner, you will probably run early on the weekend, shower and relax and have a "brunch." You'll snack on fruit and have an afternoon beer. Dinner will be your big meal, but you'll keep it under control because you have to run the next day and don't want your system all out of whack.

Your changed eating habits will be most evident when you dine with nonrunning friends. When they have hard liquor or a cocktail, you'll want wine or beer. Probably beer. They'll order steak, you'll order fish. And so on. Everybody loves a hot fudge sundae or strawberry cheesecake. The nonrunner will sop it up, or refuse it and pig out when he or she gets home. The runner will refuse it contentedly, or sop it up without guilt because the next day's workout will run it off. (See Chapter 8 for more on nutrition.)

SEX

At the end of 1981, a questionnaire appeared in *The Runner* to determine to what extent running per se and the time and energy devoted to it can influence one's sexual relationships. In a six-week period, 3,140 completed questionnaires were received. This survey form had thirty-three questions; it had to be detached from the magazine and put in an envelope and mailed at the reader's expense. All things considered, such a response indicated a nerve had been struck. The review of the finding, which appeared in the May 1982 issue, stated: "Apparently, as people become more involved with their running the nature of their sexual lives comes into question. [Our] survey provided a form of expression for those runners anxious to better examine their sexual and athletic selves."

The primary conclusion of the study's findings? To quote the article: "Runners feel that running has a positive effect on their sexual lifestyle. They say running has made them better lovers, that runners are more sexually attractive than nonrunners, and that the self-confidence they've attained through running has carried over to the sexual relationships."

There were two thrusts of thought exposed in the survey. The predominant view was that because running makes one look better and feel better, the runner is more likely to experience an improved sexual lifestyle. As Dr. Michael H. Sacks, a Cornell psychiatrist quoted in the article, states, "There's no question in my mind that people who begin to pay attention to their bodies, in moderation, develop more energy for everything, including sex."

The minority viewpoint was that because running can be so strenuous, time-consuming, and important to the individual, there results a diminished sexual life-style. As one thirty-three-year-old male survey respondent stated: "When I start training for a marathon, going from 30 to 60 miles a week, my family suffers and my wife feels I am being selfish. I am, but I still do it—I have to. I usually get cut off by my wife sexually because she gets mad."

NEGATIVE ADDICTION

The above example from the sex survey points to the phenomenon of being a compulsive runner. It is one thing to enjoy running and have it become a most important part of your life. That, indeed, is what this book is all about. However, like anything else from which one derives pleasure, there comes a point when enough is enough. When you pass that point, when you will not give up a day's workout for anything, you may have become a victim of "negative addiction." Another term used to describe the syndrome is "exercise dependency." Like other forms of addiction, you must run to feel good, to feel happy. This is dangerous.

The negative-addiction theory is not just based on speculation. Numerous cases have been documented by doctors in a variety of disciplines. Psychologists and psychiatrists have treated people for it. Podiatrists and orthopedists see the condition in the injured runners who hobble through their doors. As runners, we see it in others, and sometimes in ourselves.

Probably, the sort of person who is vulnerable to such an addiction is the sort who can become too addicted to other things—things even less inherently beneficial than running. This is a complex matter, and I don't know that there's any good way to avoid such addiction except to try to keep your running under control as you advance in fitness and ability.

One suggestion might be to race infrequently. Those who race from one weekend to the next find it hard to moderate their training, because they always must be ready to perform. If you don't have a race coming up, you tend to be more flexible toward your training.

The answers are hard to come by. Professor William Morgan of the University of Wisconsin, a leader in the field of sports psychology, has been working on negative addiction in runners for years. "We got to the point," he explains, "where we were trying to teach people to develop a strategy for coping with exercise deprivation, and we were struck with the stark reality of the value judgments involved. I'm not sure they're 'problems.'" Morgan suggests it is difficult to weigh the conflict that can be created by exercise dependency with the benefits derived from a vigorous and goal-oriented exercise program.

I have found in myself and in others like me who have been running for many years that there tends to be a cycle involved in the "addiction" element. If you do get hooked on running at the outset, there will be so many goals to shoot for—mileage, pace, racing performance, what have you— that it is easy to become consumed by the training and the conditioning effects produced by it. One thing feeds another, and before you know it you are addicted, possibly to the detriment of some other aspect of your life. This may last for a while, but eventually, because of injuries or simply experience, you become better able to keep your running in perspective.

I still love to run as much as ever, but if something causes me to miss a day, I do not feel terribly deprived or depressed.

4

How to Select the
Right Gear and Equipment

WHAT YOU NEED

One of the great things about running is that, to do it, you don't have to invest a lot of time and money in finding and buying fancy equipment. In fact there is no elaborate "equipment," at least none that is necessary. All you really need are running shoes and ample clothing. Relative to the equipment needed for other sports, running shoes, despite their escalating costs, still are rather inexpensive. Though clothing prices have gone up like everything else, you can still find quality goods at a decent price.

How much you ultimately invest in running will depend, to some extent, on how serious a runner you become (someone running seventy miles a week usually needs more than someone running thirty-five miles a week), but more so on whether you're the sort of person that goes in for creature comforts, like a running suit with a polypropylene lining or an extra pair of flashy racing shoes or a high-tech exercise bike for the basement or one of those multiuse pulse meters that can give you the balance in your checking account if you press the right buttons.

In an article in *The Runner* entitled "Cheap Thrills" (March 1983), writer Eric Olsen compared the costs of running with other sports such as swimming, cycling, tennis and downhill skiing. Canvassing people throughout these sports, he found that in tennis, for example, ". . . an average person just getting started who decides he or she likes the sport and plays three times a week" would spend $1,926 in a year. The same sort of person in downhill skiing would spend $2,894 in a year. Most runners would tend to spend a good deal less. In charting the costs of running, the article classified runners as "thrifty," "typical" and "lavish." The thrifty runner spends under $250 a year, while the typical runner spends between $250 and $1,000 and the lavish runner, possibly taking in a running tour to the Honolulu Marathon, spends more than $1,000 a year.

Though flying off to the Honolulu Marathon doesn't come under the category of "gear," if you go to run in Honolulu you'll want to look good and have the latest in attire, and that will fatten up your bill for clothing and accessories. But let's forget about Honolulu for now and try to figure out what you really need, what might be optional, what it will cost and how you'll find it.

RUNNING-SHOE CONSIDERATIONS

For most runners, two pair of training shoes and one pair of racing shoes are sufficient at any given time. Racing shoes differ from training shoes in that they are usually lighter, more flexible, and because of this also less sturdy and supportive. If you don't race, of course, you probably don't need them. If you do race, you can sometimes find training shoes that can double as racing shoes. These shoes would combine some of the supportive properties of training models with the spareness of racing models. As I'll soon explain, the right shoe for one runner can be the wrong shoe for another runner.

But first another point about racing shoes and whether you'll need them. When you're starting out you don't need them. You'll certainly not be running fast then, and you'll have enough to deal with in getting accustomed to running shoes and beginning running. But as soon as you acquire experience and confidence, I advise you to pick up a pair of racing shoes, or at least lighter-weight training shoes that can be used for faster running, even if you're not yet ready to race or as yet have no interest in it. Psychologically, racing shoes can be a boost to your running. You'll feel faster with them on, and you'll feel more like a competitor.

Two pair of training shoes are necessary, as opposed to just one, for several reasons. If the weather is foul and your shoes get wet, you'll need a dry pair for the next day. When your regular pair start to lose their firmness, particularly in the heel and outer sole, you'll want to change off. Sometimes you'll simply feel like wearing a different pair. Or when

As running-shoe technology has developed, the price has increased. This is the first $100 pair, the New Balance 990.

you're feeling minor discomforts you'll want to change off because sometimes that serves to relieve pain. Or you may find, during a change of seasons, that you're wearing thinner (or thicker) socks that work better with different shoes. (A word about socks: wear them. Only a few of the big shots don't. Anyone else who doesn't will invite blisters. Why the big shots who don't wear socks don't get blisters is a mystery to me.)

In summary, the beginning runner needs one pair of sturdy training shoes and in due time should buy a second pair. Any experienced, serious runner needs three pair: two training and one racing. If the average price of quality shoes is now about $60, that comes to $180 for the three pair per year, more if your shoes wear out and you need to replace a pair, say, every six months or so. Many longtime runners have a closetful of shoes, though only a few of those would be in active use. Runners part with worn-out shoes very reluctantly. They make for good walking-around shoes. I use mine when I wash the car.

Incidentally, when you do buy your second pair of training shoes, you'll wonder if you should stick with one brand or change brands. It is usually safer to stay with one brand but choose a different model for variety, rather than to switch brands. Basic shoe construction differs from one manufacturer to the next. If you change, you could find yourself with a shoe that does different things to your foot and stride than your original pair. You don't want that. Adidas gives a different fit from Nike, Nike gives a different fit from Saucony, and so on. At times I have switched from Nike to Asics on a regular basis, but I no longer do that. I now switch off from one Nike model to another. In the end, you'll make the best decisions for yourself through trial and error.

And that's how to go about buying shoes in the first place: through trial and error. Not a week goes by when a runner doesn't ask me which shoes he or she should buy. "Which shoes are good?" I'm asked. Or, "What's the best shoe?" I tell them this, and I strongly emphasize it to you: Shoes are different and runners are different, and no matter what you might hear about the "best" shoe or the "number one" shoe, the only way to really make the right selection is to go down to a reputable sporting-goods shop (i.e., "running store"), speak to a knowledgeable salesperson, try on several pair, test them... and decide. You sometimes have to go through several brands, at some expense, before arriving at the line that's best for you.

If you're lucky, the running store will allow you to jog around the block to test a pair of shoes. If not, you might still be able to jog, if only in place, within the store, or at least walk around in your prospective pair. Make sure you're wearing the kind of socks you run in. You want the shoes to feel snug without being tight; there should be a good half-inch space between the fronts of your toes and the toe box. You don't want any sort of pressing-in feeling at the arch. There should be no friction at the heel. As your foot hits the ground and rolls forward, there should be ample bend in the forefoot of the shoe to allow for this movement. The shoe should have a sturdy, yet flexible feel to it. Make sure you hold both shoes in your hand and inspect them carefully, as you would a new suit. There should be no imperfections in the construction.

Sometimes, no matter how much care you take in buying shoes, it takes a good week of running in a pair to determine if they're right for you. At purchase, find out if the store's policy permits you to return shoes after a few days of test runs, perhaps for a store credit or some sort of rebate toward another pair.

Shoes really are the runner's only critical possessions (clothing choices can be far more arbitrary), because they can affect the quality of your running and can serve to prevent injury or cause it, depending on many factors. It helps, when you look for shoes, to be aware of certain aspects of your physique and running style and to know the qualities in running shoes that can best accommodate your individual characteristics. You get to know these things through experience, from your podiatrist (if injury strikes), from speaking with other runners and from running publications that include articles on biomechanics and running shoes from experts in the field. It helps if these experts are podiatrists unaffiliated with a shoe company.

There are several features of running shoes to keep in mind, but, again, no "rules" to follow, because your body type and the *way* you run are like fingerprints; no one else is exactly the same. You're not going to find brand endorsement here. In a dozen years of running, over twenty-five thousand miles, I've worn a dozen brands. The shoes being turned out today are better than ever. The companies are hard at work on research and design. The market is lucrative and competition keen. The consumer benefits. Some years ago, at the start of the running boom, there might have been only a few good shoes available, but now there are fifteen or more major companies with numerous well-made models to choose from.

THE LATEST IN
RUNNING-SHOE TECHNOLOGY

It will help you to know something about shoe construction, especially with regard to your running style and emphasis. The last, or base of the shoe, can be straight in shape or curved, and while the big shots can get away with the curved, "in-flare" last, most runners are better off with the safer, straight-last shoes. A moderate curve at the arch is all right, but a radical C curve is frequently incompatible with the foot strike of the typical runner. The heel counter (the supportive wedge) should be strong and sturdy and extend from the back of the shoe toward the middle of it for extra support. Some shoes now come with reinforced wedges at the heel. This is a welcome development in running shoes. Another significant development is the insole, a cushiony, supportive insert that is found in many of today's models. These insoles give greater option for fit, because they are removable; you can use them, take them out or cut them and shape them in such a way as to accommodate your foot. The midsole, the part between the outsole and your foot, is under constant review by the shoe companies, because, as podiatrist Richard Schuster states, "It has a combination of contradictory functions," and this has brought much experimentation with the materials of which the midsole is made. In some shoes the midsole is tight and firm in one place and soft and pliable in another place. Dr. Schuster, perhaps the foremost authority on running biomechanics in America, believes that the older

RUNNING SHOE SOLE DESIGNS

Technology has much improved the outer soles, with such long-lasting materials as Vibram and Goodyear "carbon rubber" having been found to extend the life of the shoe.

New Balance.
(Steven Mark Needham)

An Adidas model.
(Steven Mark Needham)

Brooks shoe.
(Steven Mark Needham)

male runner (particularly over fifty) can benefit from shoes with a firm midsole, because, "Along with age comes the increasing likelihood of cartilage between the joints becoming less elastic," resulting in a decrease in the body's shock-absorbing mechanisms. For such runners, impact shock needs to be kept at a minimum, and firm midsoles will

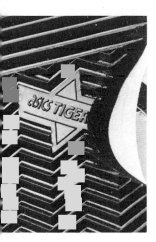

Tiger.

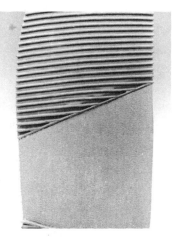

Le Coq Sportif.
(Steven Mark Needham)

Osaga.

Avia.

Avia.
(Steven Mark Needham)

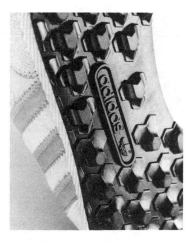

Adidas.

help. Technology has much improved the outer soles, with such long-lasting materials as Vibram and Goodyear "carbon rubber" having been found to extend the life of the shoe.

With all the improvements made by shoe companies has come a variety of options to runners. There are increasing numbers of models just for women, who in the past had to find smaller sizes in men's shoes. Women may still find the best fit and comfort in men's models, but since women are prone to certain types of injuries, such as stress fractures in the lower leg, there are women's shoes with features to guard against that. For the first time, shoe companies are making models for children that have the supportive qualities of adult models. My twelve-year-old daughter has tried them out, and they seem to be much better for her than the mass-produced sneakers found in discount stores. But then, for a kid she's a fairly serious runner. Some adult shoes, moreover, now come with reflective panels that glow in the dark, which is essential for night running.

Shoe companies have started to recognize that runners are very individualistic in the way they run, and more and more are making shoes

This shoe grouping shows the variety in heel counters and the increased support most shoes have for reduced injury. From left: Nike, Saucony, Brooks, Etonic, Reebok. *(Steven Mark Needham)*

LACING PATTERNS ALSO VARY.

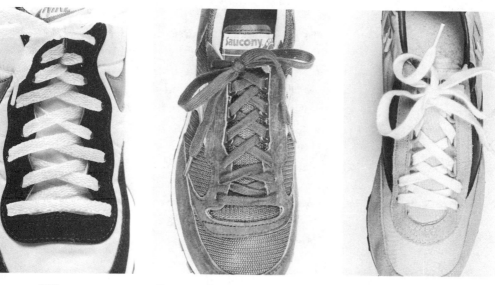

Nike   Saucony   Brooks

designed for certain types of runners, usually based on degree of running emphasis. You'll find "tech tags" along with some models that explain that a shoe is designed for the novice or the top performer or the heavier runner, for example.

Despite the revolution in shoe construction and design, many companies continue to strive for innovation. In 1985 a number of firms, including Nike and Adidas, brought out "computerized" shoes, with devices that could calculate pace, distance and stride length. In 1985 there also appeared the first shoe with a removable sole. Made by Turntec, it comes with two soles, one for hard, city running and another for dirt and other soft surfaces. The shoe retails for about ninety dollars, while replacement soles sell for fifteen dollars. Don't hesitate to purchase an expensive pair of shoes if you feel they may be better suited to your needs. What's another ten or twenty dollars when the success of your running is at stake?

CLOTHING

Throughout this book you'll see many types of running clothes. What you need and what you wear will, of course, depend primarily on the weather. Depending on where you live, there are three types of weather conditions: hot, cold and in between. In the heat you'll wear singlets (once upon a time called "tank tops") and shorts, sometimes a T-shirt, rarely any outer wear. (Over the especially sunny and warm summer of '83, I ran bare-chested for three months.) Three or four pairs of shorts and a like number of singlets is sufficient. Anklets may be more comfortable than calf-length socks. In cool, in-between conditions, T-shirts, long-sleeved as well as short-sleeved, are needed, along with cotton turtlenecks. A sweat suit, which is now called a rain suit or warm-up suit and is made of synthetic materials, is also required. Many runners have more than one. In the cold, in wind and snow and the bitter conditions of winter, there is the opportunity to attire yourself creatively for comfort and protection on the run.

In the eighties, manufacturers of running wear introduced such advanced fabrics as GORE-TEX® and polypropylene, which are lightweight and protective, and also fairly expensive. In the fall of '83 Frank Shorter Sports Wear became the first of the major manufacturers to bring out a winter running suit that combined the use of GORE-TEX® and polypropylene, the latter being used before mainly on undergarments. This new suit retailed for $209.

There are numerous accessories also available for winter use. Gloves and hats are a must. There are also scarves and face masks and reflective vests and stripings. And in the real cold, various types of leggings and long johns.

For the winter, there's a choice of two ways to go: You pick up a fancy, all-purpose running suit, and if you do you can wear it under any conditions with only a turtleneck underneath. These suits come in various sizes and colors and sometimes with matching hats and gloves, and there's no denying there are runners who care to be color-coordinated in addition to being comfortable. Or you can do what I do, and this isn't necessarily the right way, only *my* way. I rely on a beat-up, cheap-and-ordinary rain suit and put a number of layers underneath, depending on the severity of the weather. You've heard of the layered look, haven't you? My daily outfit in the 20-30 degree temperatures of the

New York City area consists of a lightweight turtleneck, a T-shirt over it, and a running suit, with hat and gloves. If it's very windy or very cold or both, I add another layer (i.e., T-shirt or long-sleeved shirt, which can be a turtleneck with the neck part cut off). In the most extreme conditions I'll add yet a fourth layer and also wear long johns, putting my shorts over them and making sure I have socks that reach up over the calves. I enjoy the snug feeling of long johns—these are the same leggings I wear when I ski. Many runners still find that the old, no-frills sweatshirts and sweatpants are sufficient. In fact, some of the running companies are starting to bring out stylized versions of the old gray outfits to appeal to more of today's runners.

By the way, it's almost unheard of nowadays for runners to actually buy T-shirts. You get complimentary T-shirts at most races, and even if you don't race you're bound to be handed a shirt for free or for a nominal "donation" at any type of running or fitness event. Every six months, I get rid of a dozen T-shirts.

RUNNING GADGETS AND HIGH-TECH EQUIPMENT

You can usually tell a runner by his or her wrist. A runner will almost always be wearing one of those digital stopwatches that have been on the market for several years and can be purchased now for less than $20. I suggest you pick one up to monitor your running. Since most runners calculate time, not distance ("I'm going out to run for an hour"), you'll need a timer to serve your needs. Casio, Timex, Cronus and Seiko are among the leading manufacturers of such watches. Some models perform a multitude of functions, and for these minicomputers you'll pay more. A stop-watch is the only gadget a runner really needs.

There are all sorts of optionals now available as well. If you run at night you'll want to glow in the dark; attach reflective stripes to your clothing if your clothing doesn't already have them. If you're a woman you'll want to consider the increasingly popular "running bra" for added support. Also, there are various little gizmos that enable you to take your pulse, compute your stride length and figure out mileage while you run.

Then there is the kind of equipment that is supposed to make you stronger or faster or fitter for running. Certain gear is used during run-

An aerobic exerciser, which enables a runner to simulate high-altitude training, a supposed benefit to conditioning.

ning, while other gear is used as an adjunct to running. There are weight gloves and other light weight products to hold while running; these are claimed to contribute to upper-body strength. There is an aerobics exerciser that you attach to the back and the mouth that is supposed to simulate the high-altitude environment associated with intensified training. There is a "gravity guidance" contraption that suspends you upside down; this is claimed to improve circulation and prevent certain types of injury. There are weight machines for home use; these are claimed to provide a total body workout (more on this in Chapter 5). There are exercise bikes that can provide an aerobic workout if bad weather or injury prevents running.

The jury is still out on the benefits (and hazards) of various types of exercise equipment as they relate to running. My advice to beginners is

Runners test the aerobic exerciser. That's Alberto Salazar on the far left.

to avoid all the hardware at the outset and concentrate exclusively on the development of a successful running program. With running alone, there is enough to deal with. In time there will be the opportunity to experiment with complementary equipment and determine if the machinery helps you to reach your running goals.

5

How to Develop Strength and Flexibility

FLEXIBILITY THROUGH STRETCHING

When I was running high school track in the early sixties, our team did a lot of stretching. Only, back then we called it calisthenics. We didn't enjoy it much, but the coach insisted we do it as part of our conditioning. It also promoted team spirit, because the whole team would do it at once, led by the team captain, who would stand before us to set an example and reprimand a slacker, not unlike an army sergeant with his drill team.

Judging by the methods proposed by today's stretching advocates, we did a lot of things wrong back then. The hallmark of our exercise series was jumping jacks, in which you bounce up and down, swinging your arms from a resting position to full extension above your head. Now this is a no-no for runners. It is known as a ballistic stretch, because of its bouncing movement, and is forbidden by stretching authorities, who contend that the jarring effect is counterproductive and can result in injury, particularly to the knees. They're probably right, so whatever stretching you ultimately do, don't do any "ballistic" exercises, in which you jump, spring or bounce —no matter how many times you see bands of football players doing it. Football players generally can do anything they want. They're a different species.

So were the guys on my high school track team. That is, we were different then, as seventeen-year-old sprinters and milers, from the runners

48

Many runners today are doing strength training, primarily for the upper body. *(Bruce Wodder)*

many of us became as adults. Those horrible jumping jacks didn't seem to hurt us any. Nor the deep knee bends. Nor any of the contorted positions the coach said were good for us. But, you see, when you're seventeen years old and running fast and playing ball in the school yard when you're not running track, you can get away with almost anything, even if you're not a football player.

We did all of our calisthenics then before doing the main segment of our workout. I don't recall ever stretching after running. Today's gurus claim the stretching you do after a workout is more important than that done before one, and some authorities even believe it's not necessary to stretch at all before running. Well, we did all right with our system in 1963. We'd jog for a half hour to start the workout (which is still a good idea), then do our calisthenics, then do our fast running, then throw up our lunch, then go home. It was neat.

Adults can't do that. Adults, even such active adults as serious runners, are naturally less flexible than kids. Aging reduces our flexibility. As a high school athlete I could palm the floor with my hands from an upright position. At twenty-five I could manage to touch my toes. Now, at thirty-eight, I can hit my ankles on a good day. (Women, it should be noted, are more flexible than men. This is terribly unfair.)

The sort of slowish running most people do actually contributes to this lessening flexibility. In the act of running, the leg muscles in use contract and strengthen, but at the same time they also shorten. Consequently, the backs of the legs—the calf and hamstring muscles—tighten; and this greatly inhibits flexibility. In addition, the relatively short stride most runners take at their relaxed pace does not help to develop the fronts of the legs—the shins and the quadriceps muscles—and so the calves and hamstrings receive the full weight of the running activity. And with little extension in the stride, the hip joints are not sufficiently taxed. What all this adds up to is a limited range of motion in the lower body.

So, one of the important benefits of a stretching program is that it can increase your range of motion. This will promote better running in general. Just as you need endurance to run well, you need range of motion, especially if you compete.

Stretching has many other benefits. According to Robert Anderson, author of *Stretching* and perhaps the leading proponent of the activity, stretching also will help you do the following: reduce muscle tension and help the body feel more relaxed; improve coordination by allowing for freer and easier movement; prevent injuries such as muscle strains; make strenuous activities like running easier because it prepares you for the stress (it is a way of signaling the muscles that are about to be used); develop body awareness; and promote circulation.

In other words, stretching will cure all that ails you. Well, maybe it will, and maybe it won't. For every fitness enthusiast who endorses it, there is one who considers it of little consequence. Among runners, there are certainly those who have never stretched a day in their lives and appear none the worse for lack of it. Even the believers have begun to question certain types of stretching exercises as being too severe for

Flexibility is important in running, as Edwin Moses demonstrates. A hurdler, Moses is far more flexible than the typical runner.

runners, based on feedback from medical people who associated certain injuries with particular stretching movements.

So what we're finding with stretching parallels what we've found in running. Generally, there's a right way and there's a wrong way, but great latitude as to how one should stretch to get the most benefit out of it for running. What works perfectly for one runner may not work well for the next.

This perverse passion over stretching probably started with Dr. George Sheehan's writing on "The Magic Six" many years ago. Running was new back then and people didn't stretch. Sheehan discovered that by adhering to a set of homemade little exercises, runners could alleviate the tightness they were finding in their muscles and possibly prevent injury.

The philosophy has not changed, but with the fitness movement currently at such an advanced state there are probably sixty stretches from which to choose when putting together your own magic six or ten or twelve. We've become flexible at trying to be flexible.

DO'S AND DON'TS OF PROPER STRETCHING

Before looking at some of the particular exercises, let's review the rules:

1. Do static, not ballistic stretching; that is, work from a stationary position and don't bounce or jump.

2. Stretch easily to the point of mild tension; it shouldn't hurt.

3. Hold a given stretch for 10-30 seconds.

4. Stretch lightly, or not at all, before running and more vigorously after running, or jog a mile first, then stretch, and then do your run.

5. Don't do weird stretches that your friends tell you to do or that you see your kids doing in gymnastics class.

6. Don't do stretches that have severely abrupt movements such as leg kicks, or you'll kick yourself afterward.

7. Consult a doctor or a physical therapist before stretching an injured muscle or tendon.

8. Don't use any contraptions that you find in the classifieds to help you stretch (a plain floor or mat will do fine, plus a wall).

9. Don't stretch too much—overstretching can be harmful too.

10. Don't expect miracles; I stretch almost every day and still can't touch my toes.

DEVELOPING A STRETCHING PROGRAM

The *Runner* publishes an annual review of the latest thinking on stretching, with a demonstration of ten specific exercises. In 1983, Royce Flippin, an associate editor, and I put together a ten-step program that included both stretching and strengthening exercises. As Flippin explained in the opening text:

> The idea behind stretching isn't too complicated: You take relatively short, tight muscles and pull on them to make them longer and looser. But runners don't always realize that there are two sides to the flexibility story—a front and a back side. All muscles in the body work in pairs. When one muscle contracts, creating a movement, the opposing muscle gives way to movement by relaxing and stretching. The contracting muscle is called the agonist, while the relaxing muscle is called the antagonist. When the motion is reversed, the muscles switch roles.

This means that when you stretch any muscle, you may be doing only half the job. For if the opposing muscle is too weak in comparison to the muscle being stretched, then the stretched muscle will lack necessary counterforce, and will tend to return to a shorter state...

Our program was designed to stretch the muscles in the backs of the legs while strengthening those in the front. We divided the body into three sections: lower leg, upper leg and upper body. These are the exercises we came up with:

Lower Leg

1. Towel Pull. Seated on the floor, extend your legs straight out in front of you and loop a small towel around the forefoot of one leg (keeping the other leg at rest), pulling the towel gently toward your body to stretch the calf. Hold for 20 seconds. Repeat with the other leg.

2. Toe Tugs. While seated, extend one leg (keeping the other at rest) and loop some sort of band or rope around the foot. This is the opposite of the towel pull in that the band should be held by someone or attached to a stationary foundation so that you can pull your toes up toward your body against the resistance, thereby strengthening the shin muscles in the front of the lower leg.

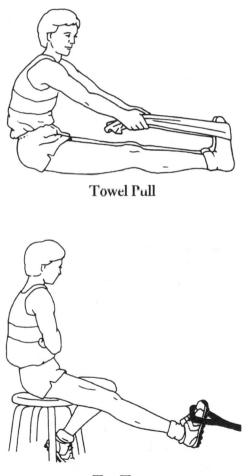

Towel Pull

Toe Tugs

Repeat ten times or more on each leg.

3. Wall Push-Up. Stand a few feet away from a bar or wall, pressing hands against it, and lean into it from your hips to stretch the back of the lower leg. Keep your heels flat on the ground. You can do this with one leg forward, strengthening one leg at a time, or with both legs back in a parallel position. Hold for 15-20 seconds.

Wall Push-Up

Upper Leg

4. Leg-Up. To stretch the upper hamstring and groin area, put one foot up on a bench or stool, bending your leg at the knee and clasping your hands around the front of your leg so it is held close to your body. Lean forward until you feel the stretch on the inside of the leg and in the buttock. Then do it with the other leg.

5. Pretzel. While seated, cross one leg over the other with the knee bent and upright, so that it is raised and several inches in front of your chest. The other leg should be extended, at rest.

Leg-Up

Then use your arms to pull the knee farther to the side and toward you. This will stretch the hip. Hold for 15 seconds. Then do the other leg.

6. Leg Lifts. Go out and buy a pair of ankle weights in a sporting goods store. They'll cost $15-20, and they'll be worth it. You'll use them to strengthen the fronts of the upper legs: the quadriceps muscles, which are terribly weak in runners and can be the root of a number of injuries. Seated on a stool or lying on the ground, alternate lifting your legs gently with two or three pounds of weights in the boots. Repeat 10-20 times on each leg. Make sure you keep your legs straight at all times.

7. Ballet Stretch. This is the preferred stretch for the hamstrings, because it puts minimal strain on the knee joints. Seated on the floor, keeping one leg extended and the other bent inward so the foot hits the thigh, grasp

Pretzel

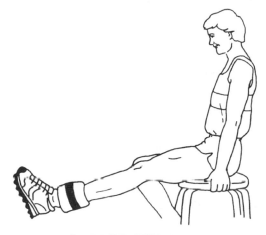

Leg Lifts

Ballet Stretch

the extended leg below the knee with both hands and lean toward the toes. Keep the back straight, leaning from the hips. Hold for 15-20 seconds.

Roll-Over

Upper Body

8. Roll-Over. Lying on your back with shoulders straight, lift the back up and roll your legs in a bent position toward your head, keeping your hands on your hips. Relax and hold for a minute. This will work on your lower back.

9. Cat Stretch. On the floor on all fours with your legs bent, lean forward in front of your knees and reach out as far as you can, extending your arms and pressing your palms to the floor. Pull back, keeping your arms stationary, until you feel the stretch in your back and shoulders. Hold for 15 seconds.

Cat Stretch

10. Elbow-Knee Sit-Up. With back to the floor and hands behind head, legs bent and feet off the ground, bring

Elbow-Knee Sit-Up

your elbows to your knees. This is a variation on the standard bent-leg sit-up, with the added stress of the feet off the ground, bringing greater effect to the stomach muscles—which work in concert with the back.

STRENGTH THROUGH WEIGHT TRAINING

The Runner's 1983 stretching review was its first to incorporate a number of strength-building exercises, reflecting the growing awareness among runners of the need to strengthen parts of the body not taxed by running. Running does not work to strengthen the upper body, but since the act of running affects the entire body, muscle tone and fitness in the arms, shoulders and torso are important.

The best way to develop the upper body for running is through some form of weight training. Indeed, weight training has become the latest rage in fitness as runners and others have discovered its benefits. Traditionalists in running have said that the way to become a better runner is to run, and never mind all this fancy stuff that doesn't include running. No doubt there are legions of top-class runners who do no weight training whatsoever. Weight-training experts such as James A. Peterson, Ph.D., contend that such athletes are successful "*in spite* of their negligence" with regard to upper-body work. Peterson says, "Everyone who participates in a physically taxing activity would benefit from a higher level of muscular fitness."

There are at least four types of equipment currently in use for weight training: 1. free weights; 2. all-in-one machines; 3. portable hand weights; and 4. weight circuits.

Free weights are the old standby and still the most popular form of weight work. This is what all athletes used until equipment became more sophisticated. It's what generated the "pumping iron" ideals of body fitness and physique. It's simple and straightforward and involves the use of barbells and dumbbells. Most people are familiar with the curls and bench presses associated with free weights.

All-in-one machines are the multiuse apparatus (e.g., Soloflex) you've seen increasingly advertised in national magazines. The reason they're advertised in national magazines is that people are buying them —otherwise the companies could not afford to advertise them in such magazines as *Playboy* and *Sports Illustrated.* And if people are buying them, there's probably something to them. These streamlined

Many runners have installed gym equipment in their homes to gain body strength.

machines, which provide resistance for a range of strength-building exercises, retail for about $500.

A friend of mine, a former track coach, has the Soloflex machine, and he swears by it. He keeps it in one corner of his basement and says he's able to get a complete workout on the apparatus in less than a half hour. It comes with a basic weight table that is attached to a post; by adjusting the machine and utilizing its various separate components, you can work on strengthening every part of the body. He demonstrated the machine for me and showed how easy it is to set up the equipment for each specific exercise. After several months of use, my buddy had the sort of physique that would make other men envious, and he says it helped him in his running as well—though he felt he had to avoid heavy running on the days on which he put in a substantial weight workout.

Portable hand weights (e.g., Heavy-hands) and various types of weight gloves are carried or worn while running (though you can use them as a form of free weight when you're not running). They're light, but typically a couple of pounds heavier when used as free weights. One of their primary features is convenience, since proponents claim that simply by running with these in hand you can develop strength, improve fitness and prevent injury. I've experimented with them but not enough to provide further testimony.

I do worry, however, about adding an element to the running move-

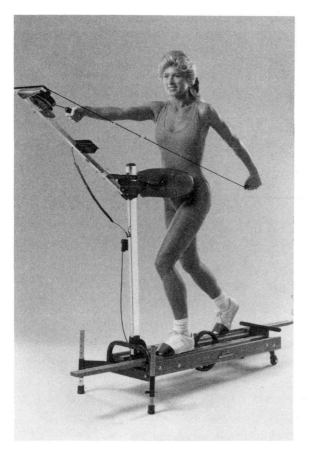

Women, as well as men, are training with exercise machines to develop their upper bodies.

ment. Running form is delicate enough—any "imbalance" can cause problems—and I'd be concerned about hand weights contributing to a problem one might be predisposed to. Yet, world-class runner Craig Virgin said use of weight gloves contributed to his second-place performance in the 1981 Boston Marathon. I'd recommend that the newer runner stay away from something like this as you're developing a running program, because your running will be enough of an experiment to deal with. Experienced runners probably could give the hand weights a try with little risk. Lately I've seen a number of runners out on the roads using them.

Weight circuits are the increasingly popular sets of exercise machines you find nowadays at fitness centers. Though free weights probably are best if you wish to body-build, pump iron and swagger around at the beach, the weight circuit, such as the Nautilus or Universal systems, is considered most advantageous for the needs of runners. Rod Dixon, Joan Benoit, Sydney Maree and Frank Shorter are among the champion runners who use Nautilus in their training.

So have I. I began a Nautilus program in the fall of 1983, and before very long I began to see some benefits. I was the typically skeptical runner. I said, "What do I need that for? I run, don't I? I'm fit. Isn't that enough?"

I was driven to Nautilus for several reasons. Finally the point registered with me that upper-body strength couldn't hurt my running, and might even help it. I could barely do ten push-ups, or open a tight jar of peanut butter. Then I decided I wanted to concentrate on the shorter running distances for a while: the mile, the 5,000 meters, maybe even the half mile. I knew that the shorter the event, the greater the need for upper-body strength. Sprinters are packed with muscle; marathoners, on the other end of the distance spectrum, needless. I'd heard that Nautilus could somehow improve flexibility, and I figured I'd try anything that could serve to loosen up my hamstrings.

But the main reason I started was that my tendency to favor the right side of my body in running was causing me more and more problems, and I needed to equalize the strength of the two sides. And finally, an unexpected reason was that I picked up a nagging knee injury and couldn't run for several weeks, and so Nautilus served as an alternate form of fitness work and as rehabilitation for the knee problem.

I am more or less the typical weight-training convert, and here's how

Two other types
of weight-train-
ing machines.

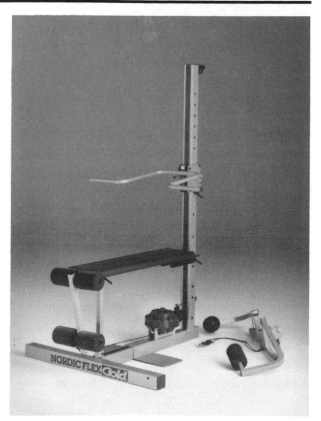

I went about taking on a Nautilus program to complement my running.

First I found a local YMCA that had Nautilus equipment, and I inquired as to how the program worked. I was told the programs were supervised by people experienced in this sort of fitness work and that records would be kept of my progress. I would be given a walk-through first on how the machines were used and what the specific goals and benefits were, and then I would be on my own, but with supervisory personnel on hand to assist if necessary. I also learned that as a runner I could have a program tailored to meet my needs. The cost was $220 for nine months (or $90 for three months), plus the $55 basic membership in the Y. This membership entitled me to free use of the pool on days when I used Nautilus. I joined.

On the first, instructional visit I saw that there was a bit of a technique to using the equipment properly and that misuse of the machines would limit their beneficial effects. This appealed to me, because there is little "technique" involved in distance running, and I saw in this an opportunity to work on skills.

I was told to try to work out three times a week for maximum benefit, and never two days in a row. Warm-up and warm-down exercises at the Y are advised, and a step-by-step set of stretches is posted for convenience. I filled out a chart and told the supervisor my particular needs. The program worked out for me was one in which the upper body was emphasized and legs de-emphasized, except for the one machine that worked the quadriceps muscles, which I needed to equalize in terms of strength.

This Y has eleven Nautilus machines. The one I need not use is that for the neck, which is the sort of thing football players love to tackle. The principle behind Nautilus is that there is a specific apparatus to work on a specific muscle (group) and that this apparatus—because of the unique cam-pulley system—provides resistance for full range of motion and is therefore a "total" workout.

What the pulley does when in operation is lift one or more metal plates, each of which provides ten pounds of resistance. For my needs as a runner, I was instructed to start with ten to twelve repetitions, lifting one to three plates. The maximum one can lift is about a dozen plates.

What I found all along was that the legwork was easy, while the upper-body work was a strain. That's the way it should be. I wasn't there to work my legs too hard. Running does that. When Frank Shorter uses Nautilus, he doesn't work his legs at all. But then, Shorter doesn't do much in the way of stretching exercises either; he's naturally flexible.

Within a couple of weeks I was put up to twenty repetitions ("reps"), which is the maximum. Stress is added by increased resistance, and within a month I was pulling three to six plates, depending on the apparatus. Incidentally, each time I attend, the supervisor on duty checks my progress chart and determines my workout, based on my needs as a runner.

It immediately became evident how weak I was in the upper body. Again, I was not there to become a muscle-beach showoff but to gain strength and tone and, if possible, flexibility, and in a "balanced" fashion to promote better running. I enjoyed the workouts as an alternate form of exercise, and with each passing week I could feel my body changing—but only slightly. It's a little like watching grass grow.

One setback I encountered early on was that because of an injury to my left knee I was told by my doctor not to use the leg-extension machine— the apparatus that builds strength in the quadriceps. That's the one machine more than any other I was there to use, but because the machine could be used only in a bent-leg manner, it inflamed the irritation in the knee. For as long as the knee was ailing, then, I continued straight-leg raises with ankle weights at home to build strength in my quads, doing three reps on the left for every two on the stronger, right leg.

I was sailing along fine through the Nautilus program until, after two months, something went wrong. I overdid it. Or shall I say the supervisor on duty instructed me to overdo it—not realizing that the more stressful session she advised for me on this particular day would constitute overdoing it. Overdoing it aggravated a back ailment (or possibly caused it), which evolved into a terribly frustrating injury that sidelined me from running, and Nautilus, for months.

From this experience I became more guarded in my approach to weight training, and I came to realize that, in a way, weight training in the eighties is like running was in the sixties and seventies for a lot of people. It's so new, so experimental, for runners, that we can't know for sure how it will affect the running body—a body that in all likelihood has not been stressed much above the waist. Furthermore, the supervisors, even the experts, are far more experienced in developing weight programs for big, bulky people such as football players, wrestlers and just regular folks who are strapping, powerful types, than for the ectomorph runners who are now passing through their doors.

Perhaps the kind of Nautilus work I was doing after six or seven weeks was tantamount to a new runner's putting in fifty miles a week after six or seven weeks. Doing that, a runner would be a sitting duck for an overuse leg injury. I guess I was a sitting duck for an overuse back injury.

SWIMMING

Another form of exercise increasingly popular among runners seeking improved upper-body strength is swimming. Aside from its abundant fitness benefits, swimming is not a weight-bearing activity, which means it will not inflict the pounding of the roads on your legs, and therefore is a form of injury prevention as well.

Swimming is considered one of the best methods to achieve overall fitness, and because it is primarily an upper-body exercise, a runner can use it to develop needed strength in that area. There are two basic approaches to swimming for upper-body fitness. You either do a number of consecutive freestyle laps of a pool, or you do sets of various strokes, in which the emphasis of the exercise is changed from lap to lap. This is the corollary of either running continuously for a period of time or breaking up the run into shorter efforts at a varied pace, possibly to include hill work.

If you're a good swimmer who has the proper technique down pat, you'll be able to acquire a sufficient workout in a routine manner. If your stroke is rough, you'll need to polish it up, perhaps with lessons. Swimming improperly will cause you to tire too quickly, preventing your upper body from achieving its desired training effect.

All too often, runners neglect the care of their bodies in terms of preparation for running. Though stretching and strengthening exercises need not become a sport in and of themselves, they should be done diligently to enhance the running experience .

6

Injuries, and What to Do About Them

The first thing you have to understand is that if you run you may get hurt. Actually, "hurt" may not be the right term. You may not feel much pain—then again, you might—but let's not talk about pain yet. Eventually you're likely to come down with an injury. This borders on fact. Ask anybody you know, who has been running for a while, if he or she has ever been injured, and the answer will probably be yes.

I can tell you that there has been one runner in all the world who has never been injured. This is my running buddy Jimmy. What is his secret? He has no secret. What he has is a running streak of ten years—that means he has run every single day for the past ten years, over three thousand six hundred days in a row. Occasionally Jimmy gets a cold. Or his stomach aches and he has to watch what he eats. That's the extent of his injury. He has also run about thirty marathons. An injury to Jimmy is feeling stiff the morning following a hard marathon.

I don't know how Jimmy does it. But he's an exception. He once did his running at three o'clock in the morning because that was the only time he could get in his workout. Jimmy doesn't have to worry about injury.

You do. So do I. In fact, I spent a good deal of my time worrying about injury. This has become a state of mind with me. I have two states of mind: when I am injured, and when I am not. When injured, I become a different person. I root for rain. If it's raining, I don't feel I'm missing that much if I'm not running because I'm injured. If it's a beautiful day, I feel I'm missing a lot; and then I'll probably run even if I'm injured and shouldn't, and make the injury worse and delay full recovery. And then I'll worry more about my injury.

Just as there are physical and mental factors that go into a running program of training and racing, there are physical and mental factors that go into injury. Success in dealing with injury depends on both.

An injury can be a frustrating thing, but now that you know you're most likely going to get one, it will be easier for you to deal with it. It's like knowing ahead of time that you're going to be punished. The surprise is gone. You can now prepare for injury. How do you prepare for injury? Basically there are two things you can do. You can resign yourself to the inevitability of injury so that when your fate arrives you will be better able to accept it and cope with it, and you can stockpile chocolate donuts. It's amazing how chocolate donuts help you get through an injury, up to a point.

WHY RUNNERS GET INJURED

It helps first to know why you'll get injured. There are three basic reasons. 1. You overdo it. 2. You make a mistake. 3. There's something inherently wrong with you, and running brings it out.

Every Runner Overdoes It

That's part of the definition of a runner. *Definition:* A runner is a person who runs and overdoes it. You overdo it, in turn, for many reasons. You enjoy running so much, you want to run as much as you can. You are competitive and want to improve your performance. You want to run every single day of your life and are not my friend Jimmy. You don't understand that rest, too, is a part of training. You are impatient and want to develop your running in a hurry. You get sucked into marathon running when you're not ready for it. You find a training schedule in a book like this and figure it's too easy for you because you played basketball in high school. And so on.

Injury does have redeeming social value. It shows you're facing up to a challenge by training hard, and in any challenge there are risks. It forces you to cut back on running, or stop altogether for a while, allowing the body much-needed recuperation. It makes you think about alternative forms of exercise, increasing the likelihood that you'll ultimately develop a more well-rounded fitness program. It makes you correct mistakes in training and fitness so that (one can hope) you won't make mistakes.

At times, severe injury can strike the runner.

But, mainly, injury is not a good thing. Injury means not running with freedom, and running with freedom is a wonderful thing. For a serious competitive runner, it can be about the most important thing there is.
How can you tell when you're overdoing it? Usually not until it's too late. That's why you're probably going to get injured. You see, we're all different. We all react differently to the act of running and the stresses of running. Doctors will tell you that, on the average, most injuries start to occur when runners exceed thirty miles a week. Well, fine, doc, but you can't race at your best on less than thirty miles a week. And here we've hit on a critical factor in injury.

Most runners do not compete. If there are 30 million people who "jog" or run in this country, only about 1 million participate in races. Those who don't compete train less, and though sooner or later they'll come down with injuries too, they won't fall into the cycle of injury. If you jog a few miles every other day and don't compete and if for whatever reason your knee starts to hurt, you'll probably stop running for as long as it takes for the knee not to hurt; then you'll resume your jogging and everything will be fine. But if you're a competitor, you'll try to "run through" your injury, because that's also part of the definition of the runner. *Definition:* A runner is a person who runs and overdoes it and tries to run through injuries.

But let's get back to overdoing it. My friend Jimmy has found that, for him, running every day for ten years is not over-doing it. For people like me, running every day for ten *days* is overdoing it. Even when I'm running well and all is fine, I have to take a day off from running once a week. Sooner or later, you find your limits—whether it involves the number of days you can run consecutively, miles per week, amount of speed work, racing frequency, what have you. It may take years to find your limitations.

You now know that it is the nature of the runner to try hard and over-do it, that in due time you will find your limit, but until that time there's a good chance you'll get injured. (And there's no guarantee you won't get injured even when you've found your limit. This relates to the runner's attitude of immortality, about which more in a minute.) Let's expand our *definition:* A runner is a person who runs, overdoes it, tries to run through injuries and thinks he (she) is immortal.

Okay, now that we have that straight, let's talk about the other two reasons for injury: mistakes and malfunction.

Mistakes

Of course, training too hard can be a mistake, but that's not what I mean here. A mistake is training in lightweight racing shoes. A mistake is running up and down the stairs of your apartment complex because the weather is bad. A mistake is trying to sprint just because you feel like it. A mistake is buying cheap running shoes without regard to quality. A mistake is not stretching, because you don't feel like it. Mistakes that can cause injury are foolish things runners do because they either don't know any better or because they're foolish. As with overdoing it, in time you learn how foolish you can afford to be.

Malfunction

This means your body works just fine for normal, everyday living, but not for running. Sports medicine is so advanced that such malfunction can usually be corrected. For example, suppose one leg is shorter than the other, even by an eighth of an inch. This is not uncommon. It can make a mess of your running, however, and must be taken care of. A sports podiatrist would probably make you a foot "appliance"—an insert of some kind to put in the shoe of your short leg, to even out the gait and foot strike. A short-leg syndrome can bring on any number of running ailments.

Unless it is quite obvious, how can you determine if something is inherently wrong with you? Only through trial and error. If you feel an injury coming on, it could be a malfunction that has triggered it. A podiatrist more so than other specialists is likely to detect an abnormality, because usually such malfunctions are biomechanical, and that's what podiatrists specialize in—biomechanics—the way you run, your posture, running form, and the like. My advice to any runner: when injured, first check with a podiatrist; even when you're not injured, have a podiatrist examine you periodically (once or twice a year) just to check out your parts. Something can be driven out of whack without your realizing it until injury strikes.

INJURY PREVENTION

I'm not going to make you feel good by saying that if you do this, that and the other thing you'll definitely not get injured. That's too presumptuous for such an inexact science as running. But you can take precautions to get fewer injuries and to make them less severe once they occur. This is analogous to life in general: you will get old, but you can live in such a way as to make the conditions associated with aging less severe (we hope).

You are *less* likely to incur a great deal of suffering from injury if you do any or all of the following:

1. Develop a running program in a graduated manner, so that you ease into the stresses of running.

2. Even when you are experienced and are running at full stride, run no more than fifty miles a week. Even world champion Mary Decker learned that she couldn't run very high mileage. And she now runs about fifty miles a week. She performs magnificently and doesn't get injured as much.

3. Don't try for a running streak. My friend Jimmy is part of the cult of runners who like to run every single day. These people can spot one another at races, and their conversation usually goes like this:

"How many days?"

"One thousand eight hundred seventy-five. How about you?"

"One thousand eight hundred seventy-six."

Don't even try for a month. It may look
great in your running diary, but believe me,
it'll backfire, and when you're sidelined
with an injury you'll kick yourself for not
taking a day off once a week.

4. Avoid the marathon. To run a marathon successfully, you'll have to advance to over fifty miles a week (see Chapter 10), and that means you'll also be in injury territory. Here again, the idea of risk comes up: when you want something bad enough, you have to be prepared to take a risk. Marathon training and racing is, among other things, a risky business.

5. Develop strength and flexibility (see Chapter 5). By becoming stronger and more flexible—with stretching exercises and weight work, for example—you can become more resistant to the types of injuries to which runners are prone.

6. Make sure you're running in high-quality running shoes that are right for you, and that when they wear down you build them up (with the various shoe-repair products available) or buy new ones. Even slight deformities in the construction of shoes can contribute to injury.

7. Taper off before races, and run lightly after races.

8. Sleep. Studies have shown that lack of sleep during periods of hard training is a symptom of injury. If you're fatigued, the body will be unable to respond properly.

9. Most of us run on hard surfaces because of convenience, and hard surfaces bring on injury because of impact shock. In time, all the pounding adds up and—bing—something starts to hurt. Try to do some of your running on dirt trails or grass.

10. Serious competitors aren't going to listen to much of this, because they're too busy training like crazy for the next race. There is hope even for these runners, however, if they structure their running programs in a way that has them peak for a select few races at a given period in the season. I recommend that you gradually build up to a point where you're racing-fit, and try to hold that fitness for competitive reasons for two months, then purposely back off from the hard running for a while. This is better than trying to be hotshot fit all year. You have to compromise. If it works, there's a good chance you'll be really fit for a few key races, then let go and be normal again before building up the next time around. In the long run (excuse the pun), it may help. Here we can learn from the world-class runners. Many of them build up so that they're in good form for the summer, because that's when the big races take place in Europe. They train firmly year-round but in a step-by-step manner for months and, finally, start to race well in, oh, June. They cut back on their training but race a lot (good training in and of itself) in July and August, then "let go" and start all over again in the fall.

Your peak season probably should be fall or spring, because of weather considerations.

WHEN INJURY STRIKES

You've heard of the Eight Stages of Man. Well, there is also a psychological phenomenon known as the Eight Stages of an Injured Runner. Here they are: Immortality, Denial, Frustration, Acceptance with Reservations, Acceptance, Irritability, Hope, Recovery. Let's run them down.

1. Immortality. When you're running well and feel fit and strong, you feel all this fuss about injury is a little exaggerated. You're not injured, and you're doing fine and racing well, and your weight is down and you feel you can take on the world. Injury? That happens to someone else.

2. Denial. When the first signs of injury occur (a little pain in the knee or stiffness in the hip or tightness in the back), you ignore it. It's something minor, it will go away, it can't be happening to you. You're simply not injured, because you don't want to be, and you go on running as though nothing has happened.

3. Frustration. The pain does not subside as you try to run through it. This is frustrating.

4. Acceptance with Reservations. Finally you give in, sort of. You realize something is wrong, but you still cling to the idea that you can run more or less normally while taking small measures to treat the injury. For example, you give up speed work for a week.

5. Acceptance. This is it. You know you have an injury, you know you can't run normally for a while (if at all), and you take steps to treat the injury.

6. Irritability. Not running normally makes you intolerably cranky. Eating chocolate donuts has its limits.

7. Hope. In time you start feeling better and see the light at the end of the tunnel. You dream of better days.

8. Recovery. You are finally able to resume running. You feel like a new person. You will forget very quickly what it feels like to be injured, and when your running is back to normal and you hear other runners complain of injury you'll say to yourself, "What's all the fuss about? I feel great."

TREATMENT OF INJURY

We finally come to the enemy. To give you a better idea of what you're up against and how you can try to get better once injury strikes, let's look at the body part by part, from the ground up.

Feet

Injury can strike any part of the foot and can be as minor as a blister and as major as a severe pain in the arch or the heel.

A blister is a collection of fluid in the outer part of the skin. It is commonly brought on by friction, such as that caused by the back of the foot rubbing against the heel of the shoe during running. That's why most runners wear socks, even in the warmest weather. Sometimes socks can cause blisters, but I feel you're more likely to encounter friction with the bare foot against the shoe. One time-honored preventive measure is to lubricate the foot with a small dab or coating of petroleum jelly (such as Vaseline). You do this to the bare foot, then put your socks on. A minor blister will frequently go away by itself and require no special care, though it might cause you to interrupt your training for a day so as not to make it worse.

For a blister that does require attention, make sure you clean the area, puncture the blister with a sterilized needle, drain the fluid and bandage the area with a sterile pad. If blisters repeat in the same spot, you may have to change your shoes or perhaps get a moderate heel lift to change the position of your foot inside the shoe, depending, of course, on where the blisters are forming.

Going from the benign to the more severe, if you feel an occasional piercing pain in the forefoot you may have a condition known as a neuroma. This occurs when the metatarsal bones squeeze the nerves in that area that run into the toes, and there results pain. Frequently this is caused by tight shoes, and so it is easy to treat. However, if it persists

Foot padding can sometimes alleviate stress and minor discomforts.

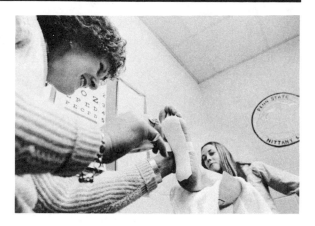

even when shoes are made loose, a physician may give you anti-inflammatory medication or cortisone shots to alleviate the condition. This is one of those hard-to-pin-down injuries that can appear and disappear unsuspected. One day you'll have it, and the next day it'll be gone.

Moving to the back of the foot, a common complaint among runners is heel pain, sometimes caused by a condition known as plantar fasciitis. The plantar fascia is a band that attaches to the heel from the arch; under the strain of running, it can become inflamed or torn. This is among the more serious running injuries. Runners who have it will complain of pain even while walking at first and will have to lay off running for a period of weeks for the condition to heal. Improper footwear or excessive training can cause it. Treatment, in addition to rest, can include heel pads or other foot "inserts," ice, aspirin or a change in running shoes. When running is resumed, it is important for one to avoid hills or any form of exercise that serves to extend the forefoot, which can aggravate the tender arch area.

Ankle

With the improvement in running shoes has come a reduction in ankle injury. The good, solid support that most shoes now provide means the foot is more stable during running, and therefore there is less of a tendency for the ankle to become twisted. Most ankle injuries are minor sprains that can be treated successfully with rest, ice and at times temporary taping of the foot so that it will be put in a fixed position during exercise. A trainer, physical therapist or doctor will know how to tape an injured ankle to expedite the healing process.

Achilles Tendon

Achilles tendinitis is another injury that has been helped a good deal by improvements in running shoes. Five and ten years ago, when running shoes were not as well made, the Achilles tendon would become stressed routinely during running.

The Achilles tendon is the strong yet vulnerable band that runs from the heel to the calf. Swelling is usually evident when the tendon is injured. This is very much an "overuse" injury, usually resulting directly from a sudden increase in mileage or speed, or a change in training such as running on hills instead of flat terrain, or running a lot after a layoff due to illness.

Rest, ice, massage and, eventually, stretching the tendon and surrounding calf muscle will help. Tightness in the area can bring on the injury, but don't stretch that part of the leg while injured. When recovered, make sure you stretch the tendon as a habit to prevent a recurrence. Achilles tendinitis frequently occurs because the tendon shortens during running and is not stretched; then its inelasticity results in injury. There are specialists who will treat the condition with an anti-inflammatory drug such as cortisone, and this can work; but use of such drugs is controversial and should be considered only as a last resort. Opponents of such drugs claim they serve to mask the symptoms, which can result in further damage once exercise is resumed.

Shin

Just about everyone has heard of shinsplints, since it has afflicted most weekend athletes in a variety of sports. However, there are various types of shinsplints that have victimized runners. The most common form results in an irritation in the front of the leg along the shinbone. This is anterior tibial shinsplints. Currently, there is a more chic form of the ailment, known as compartment syndrome, which causes pain in the muscle on the outside front of the leg.

In the first type, ice, reduced running, running on grass instead of concrete, no running and improved flexibility all help. A complete rest of two or three weeks may be necessary to eliminate the discomfort. The second type is more exotic and harder to pin down. It is also associated with tight calf muscles, among other things. When you have compartment syndrome, you feel a tight burning sensation in the muscle, and when it gets really bad you simply cannot run. It hurts too much. The reason is circulation and blood flow, which become restricted and cause pressure to build in the exercising muscle.

At its worst it can require surgery—what Mary Decker once had to relieve the pressure in the muscle for normal circulation. Most cases are far more benign. I had the injury myself and got through it by icing the area, having my orthotics ("foot inserts") adjusted, running less, running slowly, and starting my workouts by jogging a couple of miles to warm up the muscles. At no time did I have to stop running entirely.

For a while the condition was very peculiar. I'd get the muscle tightness like clockwork after one mile in a race. It would last for precisely two miles and then go away. One day, after taking the aforementioned measures, it just cleared up. It was hard to determine just what it was that I did that got rid of it.

Knee

Ah, the infamous knee! Among runners, injuries to the knee are the most common type of injury. Everyone knows of "runner's knee." But runner's knee is not an injury itself, but a catchall phrase that collectively refers to a number of knee ailments brought on by running. One of the most common is known as chondromalacia of the kneecap (patella), which sounds quite disastrous but is essentially a kneecap irritation.

Commonly, the injury is caused by a foot condition known as pronation, which means you have a particularly high arch causing the foot to pronate, or rotate, excessively upon striking the ground in running. This rotation affects the upper leg, causing the knee to twist, and in due time you wake up one day with a pain in the knee. A lot of people have this pronation; in fact it can contribute to a variety of running injuries.

The prevalence of this condition has led to a great advance in sports medicine, and a small industry in the construction of shoe inserts called "orthotics." Dr. Richard Schuster, who has pioneered the use of orthotics, has made them for me with great success. Both times, after using the custom-made appliances (which are put inside the running

These shots show Dr. Richard Schuster, one of the nation's leading sports podiatrists and a pioneer in the use of "orthotics" to treat running injury. Orthotics are used, in particular, to square off the foot strike so that the forces of running are distributed evenly up through the leg. A tilting motion at the foot strike can bring on numerous conditions, including various kinds of knee injury.

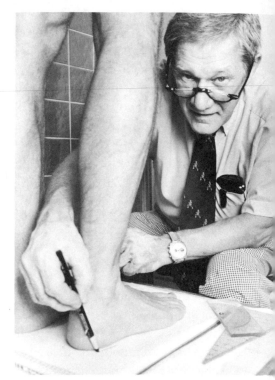

(Bill Bernstein)   *(Bill Bernstein)*

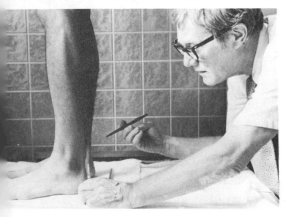

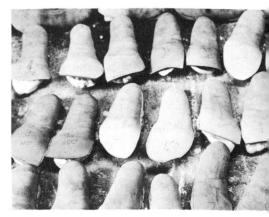

(James Joern)   *(James Joern)*

shoes), the pain in my knee disappeared. Orthotics are tricky, though; they cannot solve every running malady, and you must be careful when seeking a good sports podiatrist who will know when to prescribe them, how to make them, how to adjust them (if you complain they're still not perfect), and not charge you too much in the process. What orthotics essentially do is neutralize the foot's "abnormal" tendency so that it strikes the ground from inside the shoe in a stable manner, not in a tilted way that will throw the leg out of whack.

Doctors also advise runners to build up the quadriceps muscles, in the upper legs, because weak quads can contribute to knee problems. Since the act of running strengthens primarily the backs of the legs, you need to do some form of strength work (e.g., weight training, hill running) for the quads, in the front.

Back

The first thing to know is that if you keep the stomach strong, there's less chance of a back injury, so do bent-leg sit-ups with regularity. The second thing to know is that chiropractors who treat athletes can do wonders with runners. They are few and far between, but those that know the athletic body usually are very good. And they don't only work with the back; they know the entire anatomy, and with their experience with runners they can treat you successfully for a variety of muscle and joint ailments .

For one reason or another, including running style, you will frequently knock something out of alignment in your back. This can cause injury—to the back itself and to other parts of the body. A chiropractic manipulation will properly align your back. Chiropractors use other forms of treatment as well, including electric muscle stimulation.

For the first ten years or so of my running, I somehow managed to escape back injury. But then, suddenly, I got sciatica. Well, perhaps it was not so sudden. My chiropractor said perhaps my back problem originated years ago and had reached the point where it was an injury waiting to happen. Even if that's true, I was fairly certain the thing that triggered it was my overdoing once or twice in my Nautilus workouts.

One day I had a pain in my left hip. Then it spread to the backside and to the upper leg, then to the knee, and finally I felt it right in the lower back. The classic sciatica, my chiropractor observed. Apparently, perhaps through the Nautilus session, I knocked a couple of vertebrae askew in the back, impinging on the sciatic nerve, which feeds the leg. When I finally sought medical relief, an X ray was taken, and the condition was clearly evident there.

But, as usual, I ran through the pain at first, thinking it was probably a little irritation, nothing serious. When it persisted, I knew I needed to have it treated, and in the end I had to lay off running for a while and Nautilus for longer.

The more I learned about the condition, the more I found how prevalent it is. Apparently, my symptoms were fairly typical. Even top runners, such as road-racing champion Herb Lindsay, have had their running impaired because of lower-back ailments.

In time the condition would clear up, through repeated sessions of electric muscle stimulation, back alignment, and massage. I was also, eventually, given exercises to do to strengthen the back, and when I resumed running I did so very gradually and on soft surfaces, and kept my fingers crossed. I was extremely cautious because back problems can become chronic. Most of us know people, runners and nonrunners, who have been hospitalized with back trouble.

Stomach

The most common stomach ailment is the "stitch," a piercing tightness that can develop, during running, on the right side, left side or in the pit of the stomach. It can be mild, in which case you can usually run through it, not having to slow down or stop to find relief. The pain also can be sharp, and even then you can try to run through it; it'll hurt for a while, but the pain should eventually go away. An alternative to running through the discomfort is to slow to a jog or walk, put your hands on your hips and breathe deeply for about sixty seconds to try to loosen the cramp.

Since stitches frequently are related to eating habits, be sure to leave ample time between eating and running—most runners find they need at least two hours—and eat only easily digestible foods that would not "come back" on you during a workout. You can determine this only through trial and error, since each of us is sensitive to different types of foods. In the women's 5,000-meter race in the 1984 U.S. Olympic Trials, Julie Brown (who won) was almost forced to drop out with a stomach problem she attributed to a bowl of vegetable soup she'd had for lunch five hours earlier. She vowed to stay away from vegetable soup, at least on the day of a race.

The Blahs

No matter how much you love running and how motivated you are, there will be times when you have "the blahs," a kind of psychological "injury" that causes you to feel that running just isn't much fun. On occasion, running will seem like a chore, something you feel you have to do but don't really want to. This feeling is usually temporary. It may last a day or two, or a week or two. It can be brought on by running too much so that you become stale and overtrained, or by a rash of bad weather that makes going outdoors uninviting, or by a hectic lifestyle that makes it difficult for you to have the energy to devote proper attention to your running. When the best runners get the blahs, it is usually from racing too much; they lose the motivation to go all out one more time.

I believe it's best not to fight it. Surrender to the blahs. Run less for a while. Don't run for a day or two. Find other forms of exercise. Or, if you must run, change your workouts. Sometimes the blahs develop because of the repetitive nature of your running. Most runners do not vary their running enough. They develop routines, out of habit or necessity, and before long they're doing virtually the same workouts day in and day out. It's also good to find a new running site or trail, even if you have to go out of your way to get to it. There are times when I'll drive fifteen minutes to a park or a golf course to change my running venue, and also to give my body a break by running on softer ground.

STAYING FIT WHILE INJURED

In the early days of the running boom, many of us reinjured our feet and knees after recovery because we rushed back to running too soon after the pain went away. We were so anxious to get back to our exercise!

Nowadays that vicious cycle is less common because of the growing acceptability of exercise bikes as a vehicle to keep fit while not being able to run. Also referred to as stationary bikes, there is a wide variety of such bicycles now on the market, and more and more runners are relying on them—some even when they're not injured. The benefit of these

Exercise bikes have become very popular among runners, especially when injury strikes. You can even catch up with your reading while working out. *(Kenneth Lee)*

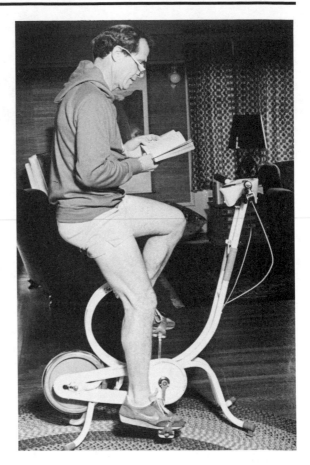

bikes is that you can get a workout without putting any weight on an injured area. If you have shinsplints, for example, you're unlikely to aggravate the condition on the bike.

By pedaling away for a half hour or forty-five minutes on an exercise bike, you can elevate your heart rate sufficiently so as to maintain cardiovascular fitness. Your leg muscles also will get a workout, though not as substantially as if you were running. A number of world-class runners, such as Grete Waitz and Frank Shorter, have expressed the value of exercise bikes during periods of injury. These bikes also provide you with your exercise "fix"—you feel better for having worked out and broken out in a sweat.

A no-frills bike will sell for about a hundred dollars, while a high-tech, fully loaded bike will set you back over a thousand dollars. Something in between, with enough gadgets to enable you to effectively control and monitor your workout, and possibly even enjoy it, is probably your best bet. They are sold at sporting goods stores and through mail-order catalogues. Check the ads in running and fitness publications.

Another excellent method of staying fit while injured is to swim. Because swimming is not a weight-bearing exercise, almost any sort of running injury you might acquire would not be adversely affected by it. With swimming you'll also get the added benefit of upper-body work, which runners need, and for certain injuries, being in the water can be a form of hydro-therapy, which expedites the healing process. As with running, you'll get more out of swimming if you can swim well. At almost any "Y," you can receive inexpensive instruction, and even when you return to running, once your injury is healed, you'll probably want to continue with swimming to round out your conditioning program.

Most good things in life come at some risk. Running is a very good thing. It is definitely worth doing, even though there's a good chance you'll eventually get hurt doing it.

7

How to Cope with the Elements and Other Unpredictable Foes

THE HEAT

On a midsummer Sunday in 1982 I was bunched with two thousand runners for the start of the Orange Classic ten-kilometer race in Middletown, New York, just north of New York City. It was hot. Very hot. There was no shade to protect us at the start, and the sun fired down on us. I later found out that the temperature even at that time, 9 A.M., was up near ninety and the humidity as well was already creeping toward ninety. Both would get into the nineties during the race. Most of the men, including me, ran without shirts and wore caps, and everyone, except perhaps a few of the elite runners such as Frank Shorter and Rod Dixon, sought water to drink or splash on themselves whenever they could.

I was fairly fit at the time, but I knew I could not nearly approach my best running on that day. I tailored my pace accordingly, but the lack of shade along the course made the conditions even more pernicious, and by about the third mile I had to do something I'd never done in a race other than a marathon: I had to stop. I couldn't run, I couldn't jog. I could barely walk. I felt dizzy. I was cooked. The heat had elevated my body temperature. Circulation was impaired. I was dehydrated, even though I was taking in fluids. Fortunately I still was in enough control of my faculties to be able to think clearly, and I could consciously halt. I walked and jogged the rest of the way, just to get to the finish, where, I learned, hundreds of runners had dropped out or taken to walking for miles. I'd never seen anything like it. People had fainted. Some were lying still in the grass. Others were drowning themselves in hose water and drinking anything they could get their hands on. Ambulances were hard at work; fortunately, no deaths occurred from the severe dehydration or sunstroke.

The people in charge of the race were not at fault. The race was well organized, the course well marked, and there were ample fluids along the route. They couldn't do much about the lack of shade; there wasn't much shade to be found in the immediate area. Perhaps they could have started the race earlier than g A.M., as some warm-weather races do (the Honolulu Marathon begins at 6 A.M., in darkness); but then, the runners coming up from the city and elsewhere might have decided not to make the trip.

The race organizers did find a solution. They changed the date. The Orange Classic is now held early in June, about as late as you can hold a

Make sure you drink plenty of water during a race. This is Joan Benoit in the '83 Boston Marathon, where she set a world record. (*Janeart*)

race in the New York area without a good chance of bad heat. It worked. In 1983 it was seasonally warm for the race, but the conditions were not extraordinary. My wife ran that day (I didn't), and she said she felt pretty good.

The heat is funny. It can play tricks on you. You can feel pretty good until, suddenly, you come to a "boil," and then you feel miserable and can become a *victim*. It happened to Alberto Salazar, the great American marathoner, some years ago at the Falmouth Road Race, on Cape Cod. The highly popular world-class race is held in mid-August, and though a nice breeze wafts in off the Atlantic and hoses are plentiful, conditions can be tough, especially for those like Salazar, who are trying to win. This particular year, when Salazar, yet to fully blossom as a champion, came close to winning, he also came close to dying. It was a hot day, and at the end of the race Salazar, who'd gone all out, was in bad shape. He was taken to the hospital, where his body temperature had risen to 107 degrees, and a priest had been summoned to his bedside just in case. Salazar was placed in an ice bath to lower his body temperature and was given fluids intravenously; soon enough, he came around.

Salazar found himself in similar difficulty after the 1982 Boston Marathon. It was a warm day and he'd run his heart out to nip Dick Beardsley, 2:08:51 to 2:08:53. It was a magnificent race, but afterward Salazar was rushed to a medical depot, where doctors again had to rehydrate him and lower his body temperature. It's fair to say Alberto Salazar does not function that well in the heat. If *he* doesn't, what chance do you have?

The heat, without a doubt, is the runner's worst enemy. And it doesn't have to be extreme for its effects to be devastating. Runners have died from the heat or suffered hyperthermia (abnormally high body temperature) even on merely warm days, when the temperature was in the seventies and the air somewhat humid.

As stated in *The Runner*, "When you're running, the competition for available blood between brain (not to mention other organs including the heart itself) and skin escalates wildly. As if that weren't enough, the stepped-up blood flow to the skin is at the same time insidiously cutting down the flow of oxygen to the working muscles by as much as one-third."

In other words, watch out. You must understand that in warm weather most runners cannot run normally, in training or racing. You can't just not run, however, and so when you do run you'll need to follow a number of precautions for protection against heat stress.

WARM-WEATHER PRECAUTIONS

1. Acclimatization. It will take time for you to simply get used to running in the heat. Depending on where you live, when the weather warms up after winter or spring, you'll probably feel somewhat sluggish and heavy and "not yourself" in training as your body takes on the stresses of the heat. It will probably take two to four weeks before your body is accustomed to the heat and you can get through a workout with some "zip."

The summer of '83 was the hottest on record in the New York area and, ironically, this was the summer in which I acclimatized best. I think perhaps it was because I didn't run that much but did run very consistently. I averaged no more than forty miles a week, but I ran six days a week. By not running a lot—by not doing any long workouts—I was never "wiped out" from the heat, necessitating any substantial recovery time. I just ran about six to eight miles a day. Very rarely did I run for over an hour. In about a month, I'd lost a few pounds, and I could go out for an hour's run on a Saturday afternoon when the temperature was 95 degrees and feel O.K. I got a good tan to boot. The moral is, Reduce your mileage in the summer for better long-term results; otherwise, if you insist on running fifteen or twenty miles at a shot once a week, you'd find yourself in a state of constant recovery all through the summer.

2. Drinking. This is the key. You must drink. In training, in racing, in general, you must drink to keep the body hydrated, because if you're dehydrated your body won't work well and certainly won't permit strenuous exercise, and this can result, as we have said, in injury and impaired health. Even on the most casual warm weather training run, you may have to find a drink (a hose, gas station, restaurant) every twenty minutes or so. I know I have to. I'll plan my summer route so as to maximize the chances of finding water. I know just where I can find an open gas station with a bathroom that has cold water on a Sunday morning. Some runners will carry plastic water bottles just in case, refilling them as needed.

If you're going to race in the heat (and for heat-sensitive runners it is not a good idea), make sure you find out about the aid stations before

It's important to grab a full cup of water. Otherwise you won't get enough fluid to keep you hydrated.

you decide on a race. One Labor Day five-miler that I ran had only two water stops. It should have had at least four—one per mile—and then plentiful liquids at the finish. It had almost nothing at the finish. I'll never run there again.

Most of us sweat much more than we realize, and what's more we don't always feel thirsty until well after our bodies have developed the need for rehydration. So the rule of thumb for racing is, Drink frequently and drink a lot, especially in a marathon. For a ten-kilometer race, I'd recommend drinking four to six ounces every mile or two, and it also helps to pour water all over you. Every chance you get, simply rinse yourself with the water available for drinking. Medical experts advise marathoners to take in a good eight ounces of liquid every couple of

Joan Benoit again. In the heat, wear lightweight clothing, such as a singlet. Men can go shirtless. *(Victor Sailer)*

miles. Most authorities say the liquid should be water for faster absorption into the system (as opposed to sugary "athletic" drinks), and it must be cold.

3. Dressing. Light colors reflect the sun's rays, which is what you want. Dark colors absorb it. Half-socks work better than full socks or calf-length socks. (No socks can lead to blisters.) Lightweight nylon shorts, the kind that feel smooth and buttery, are best. Forget the old-style gym shorts; they'll murder you in the heat. The same holds for tops: lightweight, light in color, sleeveless ("singlets"), mesh if possible. All this promotes comfort and cooling. The best lightweight summer running gear is readily available year-round. It won't come cheap. You might have to spend $25 to $30 for a shorts-and-shirt outfit. It's worth it. Find a little cap, too. It'll help. Many men will run shirtless in the summer. If it works for you, do it.

In the heat, it is most important to run conservatively, especially in competition. Here are Frank Shorter (left) and Bill Rodgers.

4. Eating. Runners tend to eat less in the summer, even though they maintain their exercise. After a workout you'll feel like drinking for hours, but you won't have an appetite for a while. It is actually an advantage to lose some weight in the summer, because, all other things being equal, the heavier runner will encounter greater heat stress. With greater body fat, you'll build up heat faster than your skinny running partner, and suffer sooner and more severely.

5. The sun. Shade can make a lot of difference, so find it. Try not to run when the sun is directly overhead. In the summer, runners will frequently change their running habits. A friend of mine, a track coach in Houston, runs at dawn or at night in Houston, where the summer is vicious. Or he comes up to New York for a while, where it's "cool."

THE COLD

Compared to the heat, the cold can be a lot of fun. As long as you dress warmly, you'll find no problem. There are no rules for drinking and fluid replacement; no reports of Alberto Salazar's collapsing in the throes of hyperthermia; no doctor's warnings about impaired circulation and your organs going wacko.

The cold is here for you to enjoy—up to a point. If you're not careful, it can give you trouble. But because the cold is not generally as mean as the heat, it's much harder to make the sort of mistakes that will threaten your running or your health. As long as you dress sensibly, don't run when it's too cold (rarely is it ever *too* cold) or too icy, and don't stray off course and find yourself in the wilderness in the middle of a snowstorm, there's little that can go wrong. Actually, the biggest day-today concern of winter is staying clear of traffic on sloppy roads and when visibility is bad. The biggest long-term concern of winter is how to maintain fitness throughout the season when foul weather is unlikely to facilitate consistent high-level training. This last factor has convinced runners of the need to seek alternative forms of exercise in winter, exercise that is enjoyable and productive in its own right and also a fine complement to running. But, before looking at alternative exercise, let's make sure you're properly prepared to venture out into the cold.

SURVIVING THE WINTER

1. What to wear. You need hats, gloves (with fingers), possibly long johns, cotton turtlenecks, high socks, sturdy running shoes with good traction, a couple of durable running suits, preferably one that is an "all-weather" kind made of GORE-TEX® that is designed for maximum protection. (See gear, Chapter 4.) Except in the most extreme conditions, three thin layers usually works: a turtleneck, T-shirt over that, and warm-up suit over that. You can get by on that even when the wind-chill factor gets the temperature close to zero. In the bitter cold, you may need one more layer and you may also be better off with some form of leggings (if you wear leggings you won't need to wear your warm-up-suit bottoms, unless you don't want people to see you in leggings). Frankly, I love the feeling of wearing skintight long underwear. When I do, I'll wear knee-length socks over it, and of course running shorts over it. With all the different colors,

In wintry conditions, you must be dressed properly; if so, you can run safely in almost any weather.

I'm probably quite a sight, but it feels good. In any case, your body heats up pretty quickly, and so even when it's really nasty, you usually don't have to wear that much. The extremities are most important. I've seen runners in a turtleneck and shorts in 20 degree weather, but with a hat and gloves. I've done it myself—in a race; and I've felt fine, sometimes overdressed if the sun was out and I ran hard.

2. How to train. There are basically two things that will adversely affect the consistency and quality of your training: wind and surface. Let's face it: if the temperature is zero, you can still run a marvelous workout. It may be too cold to sprint (cold muscles under stress are easily hurt), but how much sprinting do you usually do anyway? But if the wind is fierce, or if the ground is a mess because of snow, sleet, slush or ice, only then will training be difficult.

You have to be adaptable. Seize the opportunity of the rare good day to run faster or longer—a quality workout. On the other, typically rotten, days you'll probably have to get accustomed to less of a workout—not much more than "maintenance" running. Don't force it. You need a break from the grind of training, and many runners use winter as a period in which to let up, let old injuries finally heal, and build enthusiasm for the better running that comes with spring.

3. Indoor running. Most people are within an hour's drive of a decent indoor track. Tracks are found at high schools, colleges, Y's, fitness clubs and, on occasion, at some weird place like an airline hangar or a military armory. If you're unaccustomed to running indoors, you probably won't like it much at first. You'll have to run numerous laps to get in any decent mileage; you may be intimidated by the faster runners speeding around; you just won't feel at home. That's okay. It's better than fighting a storm, and in time you'll come to enjoy it. Most runners do.

If you can somehow manage to run indoors, I'd recommend doing it twice a week—once for an easy "distance" run of, say, five miles (could be fifty laps or more) and once for a shorter, quality workout that might include some repetition work for speed, depending on how fit you are. Make sure you learn about track etiquette —for example, the slower runners should run on the outside lane, to give the speed boys plenty of room on the inside.

4. Other indoor exercise. The fitness industry is growing by leaps and bounds, and you can find a variety of exercise opportunities at Y's and health clubs, as well as equipment you can purchase for use at home. Hal Higdon, one of America's foremost runners for the past thirty years, has had a custom-made "runner's basement" installed in his home. It contains a weight machine, an exercise bike, a treadmill and a whirlpool. It wasn't that he no longer loved running; surely he did, but like other runners, he'd come to believe in the advantages of not running now and then and instead using various alternative forms of exercise for ultimately better all-around fitness.

You can swim, ride an exercise bike, run on a treadmill, work out with weights, or do calisthenics on a home gym. World-class runner Rod Dixon of New Zealand likes to jump rope now and then and even punch the heavy bag as a prizefighter would do. Whatever you choose to do, be careful. Being fit for running doesn't mean you're necessarily fit for other things, and you must take them on gradually and in moderation—just as you took on running at first. You can never tell how your body will react to a different form of stress. Is jumping rope good for you just because Rod Dixon does it? Maybe not. Jumping up and down repeatedly is not necessarily good for the body. As with running, you will be an experiment of one.

5. Other outdoor exercise. Cross-country skiing is thought to provide the best overall total body workout, because the upper body is taxed as well as the legs and cardiovascular system. The best of the world's cross-country skiers have been found to have the highest recorded oxygen uptake levels, higher even than world-class marathoners. Hal Higdon, ever the adventurer, does it, and he says it helps him stay fit. I've yet to try it, but I have skied downhill for years, and I can

Body heat rises quickly when you run, and so when competing in the winter some runners eschew heavy clothing, though most, in road races, will wear hats and gloves.

tell you that will not do much for your running. I've also found that my fitness from running will have only a small effect on my readiness for attacking the hard slopes of Vermont.

Though I've not had much luck with running injuries, downhill skiing has never caused me an injury that prevented me from running. And I've taken my share of bad falls; everyone who skis, falls. Even Frank Shorter, who lives off his running, has skied downhill, unconcerned that a mishap might ruin his season. Shorter's an excellent skier, by the way. He was captain of the ski team in high school, giving it up competitively when he saw he had more potential in running.

Don't become too intimidated by the elements. You can gain courage and toughness as a runner by using the heat or the cold or the wind to build yourself up. If you're an experienced runner, you know that a hard run on a miserable day can boost your confidence. It also enables you to maintain consistency in training and shows you haven't succumbed to the elements. But while you're exercising in such conditions, you must also exercise common sense.

HILLS

I group hills with the heat and the cold because they are something tangible that is part of the environment that runners face and, in a way, must overcome. However, hills are also very different, because sometimes running hills can be beneficial to your training and competitive readiness.

How Hills Help

1. General training. If your regular, everyday training route is hilly, all the better. You can intensify your training at will if you drive hard up the hills, and even if you choose not to, hills will break the monotony of the flats. Over time, running on hilly terrain will make you stronger and fitter and better prepared for road racing, since most races have hills. If you're familiar with the stresses of hills and all their little quirks and nuances, you'll be better prepared to deal with them in competition, physically and mentally.

2. Specific hill training. Probably the leading proponent of hill running is world-famous coach Arthur Lydiard of New Zealand, who considers hill workouts a stage of training that offers many advantages and functions as a bridge between the aerobic high-mileage phase of conditioning and speed work, such as that done at peak fitness on a track. There are by now many variations to the Lydiard System, and hill work is only one of its components.

For hill repetitions, you simply find a nice long hill of between two hundred and eight hundred meters (depending on its grade, your fitness level and the availability of hills in your running area). After a warm-up jog of a couple of miles and stretching, run repeats of the hill in which you run hard going up, then run gently going down. (In the

When you run uphill, try to lean into the hill from your hips, and drive forward with good arm action, running on the balls of your feet.

More hill running. Notice the body lean and the running form.

ideal world, you'd get a ride down so as not to incur the negative effects of downhill running.) The number and pace of the repetitions will vary according to many factors. You'd want to do at least four repetitions for minimum benefit. Doing it on a grassy surface is a good idea; a golf course would be perfect.

Lean into the hill from your hips, keeping the torso erect, moving your arms up and back and lifting your knees. Hill repeats will give you an anaerobic training effect, serve to lengthen your stride, develop the muscles in the upper legs and possibly make you more flexible. It is a form of speed work, actually, and if done right, should prepare your body for the greater stress of running on the track, if you ever get around to that. It will also toughen you up as a competitor—although it won't help you race on the track, according to former Olympic coach Bill Bowerman, who insists, "When's the last time you saw a track with a hill on it?"

3. Racing strategy. The better runners are keenly aware of ways in which to use hills to gain a competitive advantage. Even at the middle-of-the-pack level, there are runners who will struggle up and over hills and others who will move strongly and with conviction on them, passing many runners. It's a matter, mainly, of attitude. If you're physically fit, you have to develop the mental toughness to use hills to your advantage, not let them beat you or psych you out. That's easier said than done. Running hills well comes with experience.

How Hills Hurt

1. Injuries. Any injury will be made worse by running on hills. Many times, examining a runner for a minor injury or allowing an injured runner to resume activity, the sports-medicine doctor will say, "You can run now, but avoid hills." Hills will strain just about anything that's wrong with you, so when the slightest discomfort does strike, avoid them. Hills can also cause injury, mostly downhills.

2. Downhills. In the last few years a number of the world-class runners who succeeded at the Boston Marathon came down with injuries after Boston—because of the severe downhills of the course. Grete Waitz dropped out with three miles to go in 1982 because of the downhills. Greg Meyer was hurt after winning Boston in 1983. Running downhill can have a cumulatively bad effect on your feet, knees, hips and back because of the pounding. If running uphill provides a stress, running downhill provides wallop. The impact shock of running downhill is not to be taken lightly. Be aware of it at all times.

There is a tendency to "brake" while running downhill—to pull your body back to avoid running too fast. This is bad, because it can direct added shock to the backs of the legs, making your system absorb the stresses in an uneven manner. Try to keep your body perpendicular to the hill, and hit the ground squarely so that the shock is distributed evenly up through the body. Your speed will increase, but with experience you'll gain control of the faster pace.

RUNNING IN THE DARK

Another recent advance in attire has made running at night much less dangerous than it once was. Now many garments, even most brands of shoes, come with reflective striping or patches that can be seen by approaching motorists at considerable distances. Some outfits make you glow in the dark from head to toe. This doesn't mean you can be cavalier about running at night. You are still running at a greater risk in the dark and must proceed with caution. Obviously, the better lighted the road, the better off you'll be. Use common sense, and by all means, never run in the dark without some sort of reflective clothing or accessory.

COPING WITH TRAFFIC

Tragically, a number of runners are killed every year in accidents with motorists. Sometimes it is the runner's fault; other times, they are victimized by drunk drivers. At times it's no one's fault, but bad luck that brought runner and automobile together on a slick road.

In addition to not running at night or wearing reflective clothing when they do, runners can take other precautions to avoid cars, such as: not running on very narrow roads that make it difficult for cars to pass you; always running facing the traffic; not antagonizing motorists by running in the middle of the road, in effect "daring" them to come near you; being alert when in the midst of a group of runners; running defensively at all times—which essentially means not trusting motorists. You must anticipate all the negligence drivers will show, such as looking left (but not right) and then making a quick *right* turn, or not really stopping at a stop sign.

DEALING WITH DOGS

Man's best friend is probably the runner's worst enemy. Every runner has a favorite "dog story" to tell. They make for amusing conversation, but the close calls were hardly funny when they happened.

The solution to combating stray dogs that go after runners is a simple one. Dogs, basically, are chicken. You have to let them know who's boss. If a dog starts to growl and even charges after you, there is one thing that will (usually) work: stand your ground, get mean, and instead of retreating, take the offensive. Growl back. Wave your arms in a threatening way. Run at the dog. Grab a stick. The dog will retreat. You'll see. Doing this will get your adrenalin going, and you'll likely run faster for the remainder of your workout.

This dog offensive has been proved time and again. But there are exceptions to the rule. It does not always work with a Great Dane or a large German shepherd.

8

Eat and Run:
A Skeptic's Dilemma

I've never been comfortable with the idea that the food we eat will have a great effect on our running. I know I'm nutritionally in the minority, because most runners believe that nutritional habits can make a difference in running performance. There's little proof to substantiate this, however. It's based mostly on our national obsession with food and weight loss, with cookbooks, best-selling diet books, with doctors turning up on TV to tell Jay and Dave about the latest formula to enhance everything from sexual performance to athletic performance through proper nutrition. About the only aspect of nutrition that's been proved scientifically in terms of running performance is that carbohydrate consumption in the days prior to a marathon will likely improve one's chances at running well, or at least not hitting the wall and getting "wiped out." And still you can find people, who never "load up" on carbohydrates, who run fine marathons.

The runner's reliance on nutritional dogma also stems from the proliferation of articles on eating and running found in various running publications. Many runners, I must say, seem to like doctors or exercise physiologists or nutritionists explaining their latest theories on which nutritional devices work best to help you keep trim, fit and healthy. I guess runners are no different from the rest of humanity in that regard; they want to keep trim, fit and healthy. They also want to make the most of their running, and so for them nutrition can become even more manipulative and the theories more exotic.

NUTRITION AS AN ELEMENT OF TRAINING

As an outgrowth of this new field of sports nutrition, there have developed two schools of thought, with various shades in between. One is based on instinct, the other on doctrine.

1. Instinct. Unless you are a runner with a particular medical problem, you should eat whatever you feel like, within reason, because your body's cravings will be the best determinants to your nutritional needs. This is the athletic version of simply saying, Eat a balanced diet, use common sense, don't eat hot dogs for breakfast and salami sandwiches before you go to bed, and you're likely to get all the right things into your system to nourish your normal health needs, and your needs as an active athlete as well.

2. Doctrine. Here you go by the rules, which, at various times, depending on the specialist or the diet book, include do's and don'ts on proteins, carbohydrates, fats, alcohol, caffeine, vitamins, mineral supplements, salt, sugar and so on. This is the athletic version of saying, You are what you eat, so be very careful.

The first system encourages excess, the second sacrifice. You can find accomplished runners to endorse either one. Some are strict vegetarians who wouldn't eat a bacon cheeseburger at gunpoint. Others live on junk food and are known for their disregard of supposedly sound nutrition.

To try to stimulate discussion on these two opposing philosophies, *The Runner* once asked an athlete of the junk-food school of thought to write an article on eating and running. Don Kardong, who was fourth in the 1976 Olympic marathon, was happy to do it, and it ran as a cover story, inspiring quite a debate. Don appeared on the cover of the December 1983 issue with an ice-cream sundae in hand and the headline "The Eat More and Run Better Diet."

The article caused quite a stir. Many readers wrote to say it was just the article they'd been waiting to see, an irreverent treatment of sports nutrition that admitted our weakness when it comes to food and advanced the notion that, as active people, we can eat pretty much what we please. Others castigated *The Runner* for being so irresponsible as to provide a prominent forum for such heresy. The response was about equally divided between proponents and opponents of Kardong's conclusion: "... while science spends its days carefully testing hypotheses,

I plan to spend mine eating, drinking and running merrily along, knowing that nutritional information is progressing by leaps and bounds, although probably not fast enough to save me."

Kardong stated that his diet was "eclectic and ethnically balanced," that "at meals I eat everything in sight," that he *noshes* between meals and that his weakness is ice cream. In other words, a fairly typical runner, or at least fairly typical of the way most runners (or people) would eat if they didn't feel so guilty about it.

I've seen Kardong in action. In Indianapolis for The Athletics Congress national track meet in June 1983, I went out to lunch with Don. I had a sandwich. Don had an ice-cream sundae with all the trimmings. It was bigger than a bread box.

Kardong concluded his article on the "eat-more" diet with ten rules to live by from a "nutritional agnostic." "Without ice cream," declared Rule 10, "there would be chaos and darkness."

Kardong's marathon teammates on the 1976 Olympic team, Frank Shorter and Bill Rodgers, are examples of other leading runners prone more to instinctive, rather than scientific, eating. I've broken bread with both men. First of all, their reputations as Kardong-like junk-food addicts is undeserved. Neither Shorter nor Rodgers, from what I've observed, eats very much. Occasionally they'll treat themselves to a rich dessert, but who doesn't? Besides, with all the calories they burn with upward of 120 miles a week, they need it. Though Rodgers is reputed to pig out on a diet that includes heavy doses of mayonnaise at odd hours (it's true—he'll put mayonnaise on pizza), I've seen him leave half a meal on his plate, and with the "meal" being simply a salad or sandwich. Shorter once told me that he feels nutrition is the least important of all factors generally associated with running performance.

Runners—from Shorter and Rodgers (and even Kardong) to those in the middle of the pack—tend to develop a sixth sense about food. It's like training; with experience you learn—that is, your *body* learns —what it needs, what makes it feel good, what makes it work under stress, what's too little and too much, what interferes with health in general and running in particular and what enhances it. In time you know how many hours you must leave between eating and running, what you need to drink during a hot-weather marathon, what effect (if any) alcohol consumption on Saturday night has on your running Sunday morning, and whether some new concoction your spouse whipped up for the holidays is likely to digest well enough for you to go through with your weekly speed work.

Very often you'll hear a reference to the "running lifestyle"; usually this includes eating habits. Compared to the sedentary population, runners tend to consume less food and drink in general and more of what is considered "healthy"—including those who adhere to the Kardong ethic. I stress two important points here. Sedentary people, especially those who smoke, are not in good health. They disregard positive health factors in their daily lives, and that includes nutrition. According to surveys, they eat far too much, and much of their diet contains a lot of bad things (such as fats) and not enough good things (such as complex carbohydrates). Runners, on the other hand, tend to eat a diet rich in complex carbohydrates (such as pasta), low in fat, with ample amounts of protein. They prefer chicken to beef, drink very little hard liquor, and though they like their desserts, they usually know when to stop. All told, the average serious runner has been found to consume not much more than twenty-five hundred calories a day, and when you run thirty or forty or seventy-five miles a week year-round that's not much food at all. But it's enough.

My second point is that most runners eat that way, by and large, because of the many effects running has on their systems, not because they read it in some new miracle diet book. What effects? Some are physical, others emotional.

HOW RUNNING WILL AFFECT EATING HABITS

1. Running tends to depress appetite. Experts do not agree on the reasons for this, but there is something about exertion that causes the body to want less food. This, of course, will vary with the running effort and conditions; for example, runners have reported feeling famished shortly after a long, hard run in cold weather.

2. Running will usually increase your thirst, and since you'll drink more you'll take in less food, because liquids will become a greater source of satisfaction of your total body needs.

3. Running will give you less time to think about food, less time to prepare food and less time to eat. The time spent getting ready to run, warming up, running a workout, relaxing afterward, showering, etc. may take up to two hours a day for many runners—time when you might otherwise be involved with food.

Here's what I mean. The average sedentary fellow gets up on a Sunday morning and has a big breakfast. It's the American way. He reads the papers and lounges around waiting for the football games on TV, when he'll eat some more. The runner gets up, walks around to get the kinks out, has a cup of coffee, goes to the bathroom to empty his system, glances at the paper, prepares to run, finally bolting out the door at, say, ten, for an hour's workout, maybe more. He comes back after eleven, has a drink, relaxes, glances at the papers some more, does his stretching, showers, puts on fresh clothing, and is ready for his first meal at about 1 P.M. By 1 P.M. his sedentary counterpart is on his second meal, has probably consumed over a thousand calories already and is plotting his late-afternoon snacks.

Now, the runner, too, is human and may be plotting his late-afternoon snacks, but the runner's system continues to burn calories for many hours after exercise has ceased. The football fan puts on weight. The runner also knows he has to run the next day, and the day after that, and will automatically refrain from too much food, simply out of habit.

4. Speaking of habit, that's critical to the process. We run on habit; it's a part of our lives. Everyone eats out of habit—too much so in many cases—but for runners the habits usually are good ones, because they become an extension of the training and racing.

During the week, I run on my lunch hour, because we have a shower in the office. That means I rarely "go out" for lunch. I grab a sandwich or salad after running and eat it at my desk in ten minutes after my shower. My lunch rarely consists of more than a few hundred calories. The whole process is habitual (except when I'm injured, in which case I'll gorge to ease the grief). People who eat out tend to eat far more than I do—how can they not? The typical restaurant meal is loaded with calories.

5. Runners circulate in an environment that fosters moderation in eating, because much social feedback among runners serves to reinforce the instincts runners naturally feel as active athletes. An example: You go to a race every once in a while. Whom do you see at the race? Skinny people. People who are thin and fit and good-looking. People in their fifties who look forty. People in their forties who look thirty. It's impressive. Very little food is around. There is much talk about drinking, not eating. Will there be enough water on the course? Afterward there will be liquid refreshment, not much solid food. Water, juice, beer, maybe some fruit or yogurt. After all, what are the companies that sponsor events? Companies that make water (Perrier), yogurt (Dannon), beer (Miller Lite) and so on. When's the last time a cookie maker sponsored a 10K?

This, again, is a facet of the running lifestyle.

Someone who doesn't run may instead participate in a softball league or bowling or some such thing. The social conventions of that call for eating and drinking and not much concern for good nutrition. When's the last time you saw picky eaters in a bowling alley, or in the neighborhood tavern after the game? It is these people who need to be told by doctors and other health professionals what to eat and drink, indeed how to live to promote better health.

Not us. Simply by running we know what being healthy and fit means, and, as I've stressed, the activity of running will in many ways contribute to sensible eating. We don't need too many rules. Instinctively, most of us will get to know what's best for us.

SHOULD YOU LOAD UP ON CARBOHYDRATES? AND OTHER DIETARY ISSUES

We are, like everyone else, constantly bombarded with "new" diets, misinformation regarding running and nutrition, and claims that wonder foods can lead to greater athletic performance. Herewith a few thoughts on some of the more important nutritional issues in running:

1. Carbohydrate-loading. This is one reason marathoners run marathons. For three days before the Big Day they get to eat piles of pasta, rice, breads, cereals, fruits and desserts. They're advised to adopt such a diet by physiologists whose studies have shown that a running body rich in carbohydrates is less likely to deplete glycogen (which fuels the muscles) and crash. At one time it was popular to eat mostly protein for three days before eating the carbos, but that element of the formula was found to be inadvisable, even detrimental for certain runners. Many runners probably load on carbos before a long race, or training session, without even realizing it.

2. Drinking for competition. Rehydration is most critical during long runs in warm weather because of the large amounts of body fluid lost through sweating. Most experts believe water is better than sugary "athletic" drinks, and cold water at that, because it is absorbed into the system quicker. And that's what you need: fast absorption for immediate use. Every minute counts when you're dehydrated and it's hot and you've got a lot of running ahead of you.

3. Beer and alcohol. We can virtually dismiss hard liquor, because most runners don't consume scotch or gin or vodka, for athletic reasons, if they consume it at all, and would have the common sense to know that getting drunk the night before a race or long training run is foolish. Beer is another matter entirely. Here the mind plays great tricks. Runners love beer. A lot of other people love beer too, but runners in particular love beer. Beer, for some reason, *goes* with running (a fact not lost on beer companies). Particularly after running. It tastes great, especially in warm weather. You go out and run fifteen miles on a summer Sunday, and you're bound to drink a goodly number of beers in the course of the day, in addition to a lot of other stuff. This love of beer for its taste and refreshing qualities has made runners believe it is of great nutritional value.

No-o-o-o-o ... say the experts. Drinking before a race depresses your nervous system so you cannot function properly. After a race it inhibits the release of an antidiuretic hormone, which in plain language means you'll urinate more and lose body fluid at a time when you want to retain body fluid. Moreover, a can of beer has less nutritional value than a slice of bread, according to sports nutritionist Nancy Clark. Clark also claims that all those runners who soak up the suds as part of carbo-loading are kidding themselves. She says twelve ounces of beer contains only sixteen grams of carbohydrate, as compared, say, with the thirty-nine grams of carbos in the same amount of orange juice. What's more, the carbos from beer come mostly from the alcohol and, therefore, will not be utilized for muscular energy.

Does all this mean, don't drink beer? No, it just means, don't consider it more than a cold refresher. The problem, however, is that every now and then some big shot says the six-pack he downed before the big race made the difference. Everyone made a big deal out of the fact that Frank Shorter had a few tall ones the night before his Olympic marathon victory in 1972. If the beer helped Frank at all, it was probably in relaxing him and ensuring that he got a good night's sleep.

4. Vegetarianism. Most runners eat little red meat. I spent one year eating fish and chicken but no red meat, as an experiment. I found no discernible change in my running or general health. I'm not sure I was supposed to. The question vegetarian runners have to ask is, Will I get ample amounts of all that I need to support my exercise in a vegetarian diet? The answer is yes, but because the diet is restrictive, vegetarians have to be careful in planning their meals and make sure that the vitamins found in meat (such as iron and zinc) are plentiful enough in their nonmeat regimens. Consulting a nutrition-minded health professional is probably a good precaution for prospective vegetarian runners.

Too much red meat, on the other hand, can impair athletic performance in a sport such as running and is bad for your general health as well. Numerous studies have shown that the high fat content of red meat can be hazardous to your health, and for runners in particular it is carbohydrates, not fat, that are necessary in large quantities to fuel the body properly for strenuous exercise. The running body does not need great amounts of protein, and besides, there are many sources of protein—fish and certain vegetables, for instance—other than meat. In a normal diet low in red meat, you'll still get all the protein you need.

5. Sugar. The sugars from sweets, as you no doubt know by now, are not of great benefit to you. They can't do much harm to your running; however, the old notion of quick energy from a candy bar is simply untrue. Still, when blood sugar levels drop, as a result of hard running, for example, you may tend to crave simple sugars like those found in sweets. In the summer of 1983, while on assignment in Finland at the World Championship track meet, I ran a hard thirteen miles of the Helsinki Marathon, then walked back to my hotel. With money in my pocket, I went looking for sweets, and after a big ice-cream cone and some fruity Finnish pastry I felt like a new man.

6. Salt. Though you lose some salt in sweating, your body has plenty of salt, and most foods contain salt. The typical American diet contains six to ten times the amount of salt you need. Therefore, you do not have to replace salt losses that result from exercise. Never take a salt tablet. They are potentially dangerous, because, among other hazards, they can increase your chance of developing high blood pressure.

7. Vitamins and minerals. Though certain medical authorities believe vitamin and mineral supplements are of great value, most sports nutritionists believe that a balanced diet will give a runner all the vitamins and minerals he or she needs. Consult a physician knowledgeable in sports medicine if you feel you may be lacking in a particular vitamin or mineral. Or you can obtain professional help from a registered dietician, who can analyze every bit of your food intake and determine possible deficiencies.

8. "Health" food. Real health food is a balanced diet, the kind you probably eat as a runner, not a lot of products "health food" stores try to get you to buy. Don't be misled by advertising hype and other cultural pressures to seek better fitness through wild nutritional devices.

9. Junk food. Junk food is not the opposite of "health" food. I'm not sure I know what junk food is any more. MacDonald's? Hot dogs? Pecan pie? Chocolate chip cookies? Well, in a way, yes. Too much of this sort of food is not doing you much good as a runner. But all kinds of so-called junk food are not harmful in moderation. A running buddy of mine thrives on Burger King fare, because, he says, the food goes "right through" him, giving him a good, unclogged feeling for the next day's run.

10. Caffeine. Studies by exercise physiologist Dave Costill at Ball State University have shown that caffeine (as in coffee) stimulates the release of fats from the tissues into the bloodstream. When this occurs, muscles burn fat instead of only glycogen, resulting in a slower depletion of the glycogen supply and, perhaps, a better and less stressful marathon. So a couple of cups of coffee on the morning of a marathon might help, but Costill cautions that caffeine is not an unconditional aid to marathon performance. Coffee can also have a dehydrating effect on the body, and can overstimulate you at a time when you are already anxious.

Name the one food you can think of that might be least associated with a runner's diet. Suppose you said *liver*. Pretty terrible, huh? How many runners do you know who train on liver? Well, I know of one top marathoner who once ate liver day in and day out while training for the Olympic Trials.

You guessed right: he made the team.

How important, in the end, is diet to running success? The examples of two marathon champions—runners who have reached the pinnacle of our sport—are worth comparing. America's Frank Shorter, who won the Olympic gold medal in 1972, has never been fussy with his food. He's pretty much eaten whatever's been around, keeping one eye open to make sure he's digested some of the "right" stuff. Australia's Rob de Castella, on the other hand, the 1983 world champion, is very careful with what he eats. I recall seeing him pick at his meal at a track writers luncheon prior to the 1984 Olympics, and I asked him about it afterward.

He said that when it comes to training and being at your best, every little bit helps.

9

How to Prepare for Racing

The idea of competition should not be taken lightly. It places a demand on the body and mind that will be unfamiliar to the newer runner venturing into competition for the first time. If you can handle the program outlined earlier and reach the point where you're running for four months and putting in about twenty-five miles a week, you're ready to race if you like. The primary difference between training and racing is stress. In your five miles a day you barely encounter stress, because you're probably running at a comfortable pace—which is advised, because that's the way to develop fitness and a commitment to running in the first place. At times, you may have picked up the pace just to see how it feels or because you were running with a more advanced partner. But racing will confront you with a far greater stress, depending on how you go about it.

PLANNING FOR COMPETITION

You should determine whether you wish to race, and which race it will be, at least two weeks before the day of the race. In that way, you'll have time to make adjustments in your training to be best prepared for the competition. About two weeks before the event, you'll want to run a typical workout at a faster-than-usual pace, perhaps about thirty seconds per mile faster. In other words, if you usually run, say, five miles at a nine-minute-per-mile pace, try to run five miles at an eight-thirty pace. This will bring you closer to the feeling you'll experience in the race and prepare you somewhat for the stress. It will also tell you whether you should try to run all out in the race or exercise your option to "compete" but not push too hard this first time.

You should cut down on your training, starting about three days before the race. Run less mileage, and maybe even at a slower pace, for two days, and then don't run at all the day before the race. You'll want to be fully rested. Also, try to make sure your social life is not too hectic in the week before the race. If you do have important personal and work commitments (that may be stressful in and of themselves), don't throw in a race to make things more complicated. Race another time, when you can give it the proper attention and go into it at ease.

HOW TO FIND
A SUITABLE RACE

More than likely, the race will find you. If you've been running for a while, you're likely to have come upon race notices (i.e., entry blanks) or been told about races by friends or read about upcoming events in the local running bulletins or newspapers. No matter where you live, there's a race nearby on almost any weekend of the year.

The distances most common are five miles and ten kilometers (6.2 miles). On your twenty-five miles a week, you're ready for either one. Usually the next distance above the 10K is fifteen kilometers (9.3 miles) or a straight ten-miler. Don't run those. Go for the shorter one. Ideally, find a nice five-miler. Make sure there's nothing about it that is particularly "extreme," such as excessive hills. You don't want your first race to become a survival test.

The theory behind choosing a suitable racing distance, especially for the novice runner, is that the event should not be longer than the distance you have been running comfortably in training. In that way, the added stress will come primarily in the need to test yourself at a faster pace —not to test yourself additionally with a longer, distance. In racing—and in the course of training as well—it is not advisable to add speed and distance *at once,* because that is too much for almost anyone to take. When you run longer, you don't also run faster; when you run faster, you don't also run longer. That's why I suggest that at this stage you look for a race of either five miles or ten kilometers. These distances approximate your typical training run. All you have to do then, if you choose to, is try to run it at a faster pace.

Speed drills on a track are helpful in race preparation, though new competitors should be especially careful with them. *(Tracy Frankel)*

People compete for differing reasons. There are some wacky events, such as Bay to Breakers in San Francisco, the nation's largest race, with over fifty thousand official entrants (and thousands more unofficial). *(Janeart)*

The race you find should have a field that's not too large and not too small. In a large field, say two thousand runners and up, it could be too crowded for you to run as relaxed as possible and too threatening in terms of the atmosphere; you could "get lost" in the whole thing. In too small a field, say less than a hundred, you may find that you stand out too much to suit your first-race experience, and there's also the possibility that you'll find yourself alone in the middle of the race, and that could be unsettling. Look for a race with a few hundred people; that's easy to find, because the "average" weekend five-miler probably has a few hundred entrants. A race this size also means there's a good chance that the amenities of the race— T-shirts, water on the course, mile markers, prizes, drinks afterward—will be appealing and abundant enough for even the slowest runners to capitalize on. I've seen too many races in the summer at which, with a large field, the officials ran out of water along the course.

When I want to run in a small, unpretentious race, I don't drive into New York City for a race in Central Park. The major population areas will tend to have the major races, with a cast of thousands and all the trimmings. If you want that, you'd enjoy a race like the Perrier 10K in Central Park in early spring. You'll be surrounded by runners with all the latest gear, run elbow to elbow with people for the first couple of miles and probably hear "Rocky" as you approach the finish. I've experienced more than my share of that type of event, and so I'll usually choose to run in an event in the New Jersey suburbs, where I live. I'll be able to park with no problem. There won't be a line at the bathroom, or to pick up race numbers. There won't be any celebrities or TV cameras or people trying to sell you anything. And it won't take all day, either. You just go and run and come home.

But the local race also is a risk if you're unfamiliar with it. One Labor Day weekend, I ran in a small five-miler I'd seen listed in the racing calendar of the local newspaper. I'd never run there before— and I won't ever again. The course distance was inaccurately measured. There was not enough water. The entry fee was too high. It was terrible. I vowed after that to ask around before choosing a local race. The running grapevine is reliable.

DETERMINING YOUR GOALS

Your goal can be as ambitious as trying to run the distance at a pace that is a minute or more faster than your training pace. If you train at nine minutes per mile, you can hope to race the five-miler at eight minutes per mile, or a total time of forty minutes. That's not easy; it will probably require an all-out effort.

The first thing to determine is whether you want to run through your first race at a training pace just to see what a race is all about, or whether you want to see how well you can do. Sometimes people enter races just to see if they can finish, but that happens when a runner has not been run-

Another Bay-to-Breakers shot.

ning much and decides to run the local race without much planning or deliberation. Then the goal frequently is "to see if I can finish." It may be that all finishers get their names in the local paper (especially if the local paper is a sponsor of the race, as is sometimes the case). But if you're running in a developmental fashion, you *know* you can finish the five miles, because you've done it regularly in training. What you don't know is how fast you can run it, and that's primarily why you've entered a race.

If you train at, say, a ten-minute pace (or ten minutes per mile), you may be wondering how you can expect to run at a nine-minute pace in the race, especially since you've not had even a taste of speed work — that is, fast-paced training. Your training pace is casual and unpressed; you have a lot more to give if you want. But be prepared to experience "hard feelings" you haven't experienced in years.

To play it safe, yet have a formidable goal, you may want to shoot for a pace that is between thirty seconds and a minute faster than your usual pace. If you've been running at least twenty-five miles a week and have been at it for a period of months, you've come to know yourself and your body and are in the best position to determine what to shoot for. Your goal must be accessible, because if it isn't, you could experience too much physical difficulty during the race and then too much emotional stress afterward. Whereas, if you are realistic, not *only* will you have the satisfaction of performing up to or above expectations, but the experience will enhance your future running efforts as well.

My wife is a good example of the typical runner (and I'll use her from time to time to illustrate a point). When she began her running some years ago, her pace was over 10 minutes per mile. In her first race, a four-miler, she ran 38:30, a pace of about 9:37 per mile. Now her training pace is about 9 minutes per mile, and her best time for five miles is 39:30, or just under 8 minutes per mile.

BEFORE THE RACE

Though a long-distance race such as a marathon requires a prescribed "method" of eating in the days leading up to the race, a five-miler or a 10K does not. In fact, you would not want to eat any differently or attempt any sort of nutritional experimentation, because that could change the way your system reacts to running, and adversely affect your race. Just don't eat too much of a dinner the night before; you don't want to have a bloated feeling in the morning. Most races are held in the morning, and most runners find that eating little or nothing prior to the event is the best approach, depending on the starting time.

A typical prerace "meal" for a race of this type is simply toast and tea or coffee, eaten at least two hours before the start. If the race is in the afternoon you'll have to plan accordingly, eating a morning meal that you can digest properly for your midday event.

On a warm day, you'll need to be fully hydrated, so plan on drinking at least twelve ounces of water before a morning race, even close to the starting time. Don't worry about the liquid causing discomfort during the race, because the kidneys "shut down" for a period when you run and you won't have to pull to the side of the road for an emergency pit stop. You'll also want to drink a cup of water every mile or so on a warm day.

You must arrive at the race site a good hour before the scheduled start. You'll have to check in and get your number (and maybe enter if you haven't done that already), familiarize yourself with the course, warm up,

Ed Moses demonstrates certain stretches that are good for a prerace warm-up.

use the bathroom (and sometimes wait on line to use it) and have a few minutes after all that to do nothing but relax and mentally prepare for the race. Rushing through this can be terribly unsettling. On occasion, you have to wait on line simply to get your number; the possibility of lines for everything is another good reason to find a relatively small race.

The warm-up is critical. Don't listen to anyone who tells you the race is enough of a workout, so why also run a warm-up. The point is that to put in a harder-than usual effort, your body has to be, well, warmed up. Jog at least a mile about a half hour before the race; then do your

Make sure your shoelaces are tied tightly before you race. *(Jeff Johnson)*

stretching exercises; then jog a bit more; then stretch a bit more; then do a few wind sprints (fifty yards will do). Then relax for fifteen minutes. Then you'll be ready to race.

Make sure to bring along with you such things as Vaseline, extra shoelaces, safety pins (for your numbers, in case the race people run out) and a change of clothing. It won't hurt to have a second pair of running shoes along as well, in case something unexpected suddenly happens to your first pair, such as a cracked heel cup or a dislodged sole or anything that makes it hazardous to wear them in competition. Before the start of the race, be sure your shoes are tightly tied.

Mental training is receiving a lot of attention in sports nowadays, especially in individual sports such as running. Prior to the race, review your training and your strategy, imagine yourself during the race, think positively of how well prepared you are—in other words, try to be as secure and confident as possible. If you can achieve that, it will help.

RACE STRATEGY

Your strategy begins when you line up at the start. No matter what the size of the field or the distance, there is always a pecking order: the fastest runners stand at the front, and the slower runners stand at the back. Sometimes race officials will direct you where to line up, but even if they don't, you can figure it out for yourself. Be conservative. You don't want to be trampled, and this can happen even in a small field, because runners tend to start out very fast. So stand somewhere in the middle, or even near the back if necessary.

You should be wearing a stopwatch to monitor your pace (let's hope the miles will be marked off or called out); you'll want to run at an even

In a crowded race (and most are crowded), it's important to get good position at the start so you can run unimpeded once the gun sounds. For your first race, try to place yourself in the middle of the pack so that you won't get trampled by the faster runners.

pace all the way through. An even pace will usually yield the best results and deal out the least amount of stress. Many runners will run their first mile at a high speed, then slow down and "fight" it the rest of the way. I know; I've done that too many times myself. In the excitement and anxiety of the start, it's easy to get drawn into the fast pace of those around you. Knowing just how fast to go out will come with experience. As a beginner, avoid this temptation. Run at your own pace. I can tell almost to the second how fast I'm running, because I know how my body feels at various paces.

Shoot for your "even" pace and try to stay with it. It will be perfectly natural for you to start to feel a little tight and pressed after two or three miles, especially when you're new to competition. At racing pace, your body's needs will increase—the need to take in and circulate oxygen, the

In a race, you want to get good leg extension and run smoothly, keeping the body erect and arms moving up and back so you won't tighten up— as shown by Lasse Viren of Finland and Carlos Lopes of Portugal in the 1976 Olympic 10,000. *(Paul Sutton/DUOMO)*

In road racing, you have to be prepared to race around curves and corners. You have to cut in so you run the shortest possible distance.

need to pump blood, the need to recruit muscle fibers—and these needs can be filled only up to a point. After that, it gets harder and harder to run at your desired pace, and then fatigue sets in, and for a portion of the race you'll experience a vague sort of nagging discomfort. This is when mental ability joins with physical training to produce a controlled effort. As long as you haven't run recklessly fast at any point, you'll be able to hold on and avoid giving in to the discomfort. Try to get good leg extension, keeping your body erect and your arms moving so that you won't tighten up. Try not to allow your running form to change; try to be smooth; try to walk your way through the difficult stages. You may have to slow your pace a little. Try to run the shortest distance around corners.

All of this is experimentation anyway. Just as your initial miles in training were an experiment and you learned how to cope with stress and develop as a runner, the same applies to competition. It takes many races to acquire the sense and savvy to be a capable competitor. Try to hold your pace and form for as long as you can, ultimately to the finish if possible. At the finish, if you've put in a hard, honest effort you'll feel woozy and spent, but "good."

RACE RECOVERY

Depending on the weather, find a tall drink, change to a dry shirt, put on your sweats, walk around, calm down and, before too long, run some more. That is, take your warm-down run—a mile, maybe two, of easy jogging so your system will come to a gradual stop. Stretch as well.

You probably won't have much of an appetite for a while, but when you do you'll be quite hungry. Have a good, solid postrace meal (whatever you feel like eating usually will be "right"), and if you feel tired later in the day, treat yourself to a nap; you've earned it.

The next day, you'll feel tight and heavy in the legs, particularly in the backs of the legs (hamstrings). There might also be some localized soreness. Apply an ice pack to any soreness as soon as possible, and ice the area twice a day until relief is evident. It might take three or four days to feel normal again, depending on how hard an effort you put into your first race. As soon as you feel yourself again, you'll probably feel better than ever about your running and will want to plan for future competition. Before you do that, you need to evaluate your first performance.

EVALUATING YOUR PERFORMANCE

For a first race, this need not require much analysis. As I've said, you've gone through an experiment. Think about your mile "splits" (time) and how closely you hit your desired pace; how you felt along the way; how you felt at the finish and in the days after; how close you came to running all out—that is, your perceived effort; how you felt about the experience of being in a race with your peers; how you felt about testing yourself, and to what extent you'd want competition, at this stage, to be a part of your running program. Don't evaluate your race in terms of success and failure. There can be no success or failure in a first race (or perhaps even in a second or third, for that matter). You are defining, as you take on races, what your competitive abilities and efforts are to be. You can't yet say you've succeeded or failed. If at first you did not meet your goals, it is probably because your goals were too great. But you couldn't really know that until you'd tried. Perhaps your goal of a nine-minute pace, for example, should have been nine-thirty. Okay, you've learned something about yourself and the running process.

A race evaluation, then, is not to say whether you ran a good or a bad

Another major race, the Gasparilla 15K in Tampa, Florida.

race, at this point. It is to review the whole experience of the race, determine how you felt about the whole thing, figure out what you learned from it, and decide whether you want to do it again. It is sometimes best not to make that decision immediately, because in the stressful aftermath of competition, one's judgments are not always reasoned. Wait a few days, or even weeks, before deciding whether you want to race again. Most likely you will (though if you don't, remember that your running program can still be rich and fulfilling).

TRAINING FOR FUTURE COMPETITION

Where do you go from here? It is now time to think in the long term for training and racing—for the success of your running program in general and in case you decide at some point that you'd like to give the marathon a try.

Theoretically, by now you have run for four months and have competed in your first race. What follows now is a general program for the next eight months, designed to keep you racing-fit and develop your conditioning to the point where you could advance to half-marathon or marathon preparation if you chose to. Remember that your mileage going into your fifth month is roughly twenty-five miles a week. So...

Month 5

Continue to run about twenty-five miles a week. Your mission will be to fully recover from your first race and sink back into regular training full of zeal and injury-free. Suppress the urge to run any more than that until your sixth month.

Month 6

Increase gradually to thirty miles a week by the end of the month. Try to do that on five days of running a week. In the middle of the month, find a local race, but instead of running the main race, enter the one- mile "fun run"—just for fun. Try your best, but don't go into it with any sort of do-or-die mentality. Such a short distance will be another type of race experience and will give you more of a feeling for speed. You must do a very substantial warm-up prior to such a speed race.

Month 7

Increase gradually to thirty-five miles a week by the end of the month. Run this on five days of running per week. Try two new things during this month: 1. make one of your weekly workouts a faster-paced run over a short distance (say a "hard" three miles), and 2. make one of your weekly runs (preferably on the weekend) a slower-paced run over a longer distance (say an "easy" eight to ten miles). Now, after six months of running, you are beginning to work on the training "mix." Continue with this mix on a regular basis.

Month 8

Increase gradually to forty miles a week by the end of the month. Start to run six days a week, if possible, though don't be a slave to that, because then the running compulsion will get the best of you. Try to find a race, a 10K (if you first ran a five-miler, and vice versa if your first race was a 10K), for the end of the month.

Month 9

Continue to run forty miles a week, six days a week. Concentrate on training consistency.

Month 10

Continue to run forty miles a week. Try to find a live-mile race for the end of the month. You should be able to run it a good deal faster than your first five-miler, six months before, providing the conditions are not extreme (such as hot weather). If you find your time is not faster, you're doing something wrong. Most likely, it would be that you haven't allowed for proper rest prior to the race. It's important to start reducing your normal training load a couple of days before a race. Many runners (including me) do no running whatsoever the day before, finding it leaves us fresh and full of desire on race day.

Month 11

Increase gradually to forty-five miles a week by the end of the month. Find another one-mile fun run and try to run it faster than your first one. Don't do your "speed" workout on the week of your mile race.

Month 12

Continue to run forty-five miles a week. Try to run a longer-distance race at the end of the month, not more than a half-marathon. Whatever distance you find, you should not go into it with the idea of racing it as hard as you have a five-miler or a 10K. Try to run it faster than training pace, but only for the experience. If you find a half-marathon, you

RACE PACE CHART

Most runners use their pace per mile to gauge their progress. This chart will help you determine realistic racing goals.

PACE PER MILE	3 miles	5 miles	10 kilometers
	Total Time		
6:00	18:00	30:00	37: 17
6:15	18:45	31 :15	38:50
6:30	19:30	32:30	40:23
6:45	20:15	33:45	41 :57
7:00	21 :00	35:00	43:30
7:15	21 :45	36:15	45:03
7:30	22:30	37:30	46:36
7:45	23:15	38:45	48:09
8:00	24:00	40:00	49:43
8:15	24:45	41:15	51:16
8:30	25:30	42:30	52:49
8:45	26:15	43:45	54:22
9:00	27:00	45:00	55:55
9:15	27:45	46:15	57:28
9:30	28:30	47:30	59:02
9:45	29:15	48:45	60:35
10:00	30:00	50:00	62:09
10:15	30:45	51:15	63:42
10:30	31:30	52:30	65:15
10:45	32:15	53:45	66:48
11 :00	33:00	55:00	68:21
11 :15	33:45	56:15	69:54
11 :30	34:30	57:30	71 :27
11 :45	35:15	58:45	73:00

would do well to run it at training pace, since it would probably be the longest run of your life, by a good three miles. If you run it smoothly and it doesn't "wipe you out," you've clearly succeeded.

Speed Work

Though you have been doing some faster-paced runs, and raced a few quick one-milers, you have not yet done any real speed work. Speed work is extremely beneficial to racing performance, but it can also place an extraordinary demand on the body. That is why I don't recommend speed work for most new runners until they have been running for a year or so. Speed work is enhanced by one's general conditioning, which is not amply developed in many runners until they've been training consistently for several months.

But some runners adapt to training faster than others, and if you feel you are one of those accelerated runners, you can experiment with speed work after, perhaps, six months of running and with a couple of races under your belt.

To keep such speed work as simple as possible for now, just go to the nearest track and try the following: **1.** Jog one mile; **2.** stretch; **3.** run one quarter-mile lap fast, at a pace of roughly ten seconds per mile faster than your five-mile racing pace (if you race five miles in forty-five minutes, or nine-minute pace, your quarter-mile lap should be done in about two minutes); **4.** jog a lap, walking part of it if you feel like it. **5.** Depending on how you feel, repeat the fast-and-slow laps so that you've done a total of eight to ten total laps (half fast, half slow).**6.** Jog one mile; **7.** stretch. **8.** Run very easily, if at all, the next day.

You've run for a full year. You're running almost every day. You're putting in over forty miles a week. You've raced. You've lost weight; you feel great. You're a new person. You get some crazy idea that you might like to run a marathon. But before you get too serious about that, treat yourself to one of those $200 all-weather, all-everything running suits. And take a couple of days off from running. You'll feel even better.

10

How to Prepare
For Your First Marathon

The experience of the marathon is commonly spoken about in mystical terms, as though it were some sort of exploration into space or otherworld adventure into forbidden territory. In a way, it is. You can't be too cautious about the marathon. You can never really be sure if you're fully prepared for one. Much is left to chance— the weather, one way or another, can make all the difference. It was not too long ago when the few people running marathons were accomplished distance-*men* moving up from the 10,000 meters. Today's hordes of running-boomers enter the once-restricted territory of the top runner when they enter a marathon, and that's why the marathon in some corners is thought to be a risky venture that can provide agony or ecstasy—both at the same time in some cases.

But you should not feel too apprehensive. You've come this far, you're a committed runner, you can run half a marathon with little difficulty (an accomplishment in and of itself), you have heard about how "great" and "challenging" a marathon can be, and you want to see for yourself. Good. Just don't go into it for the wrong reasons, don't take it lightly, and be well prepared for hitches along the way.

MAKING THE COMMITMENT

For a first-time marathon hopeful, the approach is a simple one. It is based primarily on arithmetic. Almost anyone can be trained to run

The strain of the marathon shows on these two top runners. *(Steve Sutton/DUOMO)*

twenty miles. You can probably run twenty miles right now. If you've been running for a year, run forty-five miles a week and have run thirteen miles in a race, believe me, if you wanted to, you could go and eke out twenty miles. You might have to push through the last couple of miles, but you'd make it. And you'd feel great for having been able to do it.

But the marathon, as every runner knows, is twenty-six miles 385 yards. That's what makes the marathon the *marathon.* You see, God gave us bodies that could store enough fuel to take us twenty miles fairly comfortably, but beyond twenty ... we're on our own. That means we have to somehow trick our bodies into managing to handle the greater distance.

The trick is to run a lot. There's no two ways about it. You've got to do a lot of running for weeks on end to condition the body for a run of 26.2 miles.

The stress of competition applies to the marathon in a different way. In a five-mile race, you feel a heavy, intense sort of stress early in the race, as you run close to the "edge" and then push through it. In the marathon, for the newer runner, the stress is far more gradual, but once it hits you with its full force, it's much more vicious and debilitating. You can "stroll" through the first fifteen miles of a marathon, and find the next five miles only a bit more stressful, and then—pow—at twenty or twenty-one miles, you "hit the wall."

You must respect the wall, that point beyond twenty miles when your God-given body is not supposed to be running. If you don't respect it, the wall can chew you up and spit you out, leaving you feeling worse than you've ever felt in your entire life. That is why all of your training and racing must be devised with the wall in mind. You must be prepared to venture beyond twenty miles in a marathon with the least possible risk of smashing into the wall. People do it. Thousands do it. It's hardly impossible. You can do it. Let's find out how to go about it.

If you can take a hint, you realize by now that I do not believe every runner should venture into the marathon. The commitment is great, and you must determine first if it is worth it. On paper it is easy to say you'll do all this running day in and day out for months, but detours can ruin the best-laid plans. So why are so many thousands of runners popping up in marathons all over the country—so many that a number of events have instituted entry procedures to limit the size of their fields? The main reason is the challenge and the glory; to see if they can do it. Doing it, for some, means to finish; for others, it means to finish in a particular time. There are a host of reasons, but the opportunity to meet the challenge is, I think, the most compelling one.

Most people in their daily lives have little opportunity to test themselves on their own, little chance to shoot for a difficult goal and go about reaching it all by themselves—and then have a concrete yardstick by which to judge whether or not they succeeded. The marathon provides that for people, and if you're a runner it's hard not to want to experience that. When it works (and when you train sensibly it usually does), it can truly be one of life's peak experiences. Believe me, if you run and finish a marathon, you'll feel wonderful about it. For an earlier book of mine on marathon running, I conducted a survey to determine why so many runners were getting hooked on the marathon, and the vast majority of the respondents said they needed the challenge. Going for it added a fulfilling component to their lives.

Think hard about this, and if you decide you want to pursue it, give yourself six months to prepare specifically for your first marathon. It will take that long for your training to advance from the forty to forty-five miles you've just reached after a year to marathon fitness.

CHOOSING A RACE

This may seem like putting the cart before the horse. But before you can calculate your training needs and figure out exactly how long you'll have to get ready, you need to have your race determined. This will also put your mind at ease; it will be one less thing to worry about. So find your race, and enter it. And barring an unforeseen detour, stay with the race. Don't change your mind every so often because of what you hear about other races through the running grapevine. Make a commitment to your race in the same way you'll have to make a commitment to your training.

Choice of race is critical. Obviously, for a first marathon you'll want to look for an easy race. Understand this; there is no such thing as an "easy" marathon. Running twenty-six miles is hard, no matter where and when you do it. There are easier marathons. You don't want one with a lot of hills (though a pancake-flat course is not always best) or one held at high altitude (unless you live at high altitude) or one held in warm weather.

Eliminating those conditions, there are still a few hundred marathons to choose from in the United States. I also advise against making a trip for your first marathon. Too hectic. Find one you can drive to in a few hours the day before or two days before. Within two hundred miles of your home there should be an ample selection. So if you live in Dallas,

You have to try to concentrate in the latter stages of a marathon. If you're well trained, you should be able to break through the "wall."

don't plan on running the New York Marathon (assuming you can get in) as your first. Run the Dallas White Rock Marathon.

Choice of marathon usually boils down to choosing between a high-powered, major, big-city event with several thousand runners, and a small, local affair of the sort that existed years ago when marathon runners were considered, as Frank Shorter has said, weird people with strange daily habits. Each type will provide a different experience. One is not "better" than the other. It depends on your temperament and what you want out of the experience of a first marathon.

If you want to run it in relative privacy and not see your name in the papers or find yourself elbow to elbow with world-class runners at a prerace pasta party or at the starting line with what appears to be every runner in the known universe, then a small, unpretentious race is for you. You can roll into town the night before, find a motel room with no problem, park near the starting line, not have TV Minicams following you to the bathroom, and so on. It also means you probably won't get a bagful of goodies at the finish and have a lot of medical people around to tend to your every ache, either.

Sometimes you can find the best of both worlds: a marathon that gives you a little TLC and attention but enables you as well to avoid a lot of fuss and commotion if you want to. To help you decide which sort of marathon appeals to you, look through the various lists of marathons currently run (see Appendix I). You'll also find such lists in the running magazines, and they're usually accompanied with information on how the events are conducted. *The Runner* carries a monthly race calendar and an annual marathon listing with about three hundred events. *Running Times,* which is made up mainly of race listings, is a more comprehensive source for such information.

The best way to get a fix on the various races might be to send a Xeroxed entry request to a couple of dozen races. The entry blanks will list all the race details, so by scanning those, you can see which you prefer. After you have your race picked out, you can accelerate your training. And that's one thing that will keep you motivated: thinking about the race, what it's like, the course, and imagining yourself running it. All that is part of the training, as a matter of fact.

PRERACE PREPARATION

Training: Stage II

You've already done Stage I—if you've been running for a year and have reached the level of forty to forty-five miles a week. Stage I is the first year of fitness, to get to the point where you can advance into more strenuous training. If you're not there yet, go back to the earlier chapters to find out how to get through the first year.

Stage II takes about three months. You need to accomplish two things here: increased mileage overall and the long-run habit. They will go together.

Month 1

Run a minimum of forty-five miles a week during this month. The habit of running a longer weekend run should be continued so that at the end of the month you can run twelve miles comfortably. You'll probably have to be running six days a week at this point.

Month 2

You should be running fifty miles a week by the end of this month. Your long run should be fourteen miles. Find a 10K race and run it hard. Allow time to taper off for it and recover after it. Don't train "through" it. It will mean a bit of a loss in mileage for a few days, but the speed of the race will be good for you, and the opportunity to compete will be motivating. In all likelihood, you'll set a PR (personal record) for the 10K.

Month 3

Continue to run fifty miles a week. If you can manage this training load for several weeks, you're doing great. Your long run should be sixteen miles by the end of the month. Sometime during the month, find a mile fun run and race it, but this time train through it; don't cut your mileage back just for that. You'll probably earn another PR, and again, the faster running will do you some good.

Training: Stage III

In this final stage you'll continue to combine consistent training with long runs and racing, but at an increasingly greater intensity. Watch out for minor aches and soreness, because they can signal the onset of injury. Better to cut back here and there than to gamble, get hurt and ruin everything.

At Honolulu, it's so warm that they start the race at 6 A.M., in darkness, so the runners won't have to run in the heat of the day. New runners should not venture into a marathon run on a hot day.

Month 4

First run easy for a week. After building to several weeks of fifty miles a week and a long run of sixteen miles, your system needs a break, and that, too, is part of the training mix: rest. By rest in this case I mean a week's running of thirty miles, including only a weekend "long" run of less than ten miles. Mentally you'll feel guilty that you're not running more, but physically you will be gaining from the respite. And don't worry about the two pounds you may gain; you'll run it off soon enough. After the easy week, resume fifty miles a week and get the total to fifty-five by the end of the month, by which time your longest run should be eighteen miles.

Month 5

Continue to run fifty-five miles a week, and increase your long run so that you run your first 20-mile workout six weeks before the marathon. The week after your first twenty, go back to running no more than fifteen miles as your long run, and alternate weeks of medium-long runs (about fifteen miles) and long runs (about twenty) for the rest of the month's training, making sure you run no more than ten to thirteen miles on your long run the week before the marathon. A series of long runs would look like this:

> 6 weeks before: 20 miles
>
> 5 weeks before: 15 miles
>
> 4 weeks before: half-marathon race (not necessary to go all out)
>
> 3 weeks before: 20 miles
>
> 2 weeks before: 15-20 miles
>
> 1 week before: 10-13 miles

Month 6 (the Last Month)

Continue to run fifty-five miles and nudge up to sixty for a week or two in your final push toward optimum fitness. If you run a half-marathon, it should be done no less than three weeks before the marathon. Beginning ten days or so before the marathon, start to taper off. Run a few miles or so less than usual for a few days, and then, in the last week, run only a few miles a day, then take a day or two with no running, before the race.

Your final week might look like this: Sunday: ten to twelve miles; Monday: seven miles; Tuesday: six miles; Wednesday: five miles; Thursday: three miles; Friday: no running; Saturday: no running; Sunday: the marathon.

Many new runners wonder how they'll be able to run the twenty-six miles of a marathon if they haven't run twenty-six miles in training—and why they're not advised to run that far in training. An effort of twenty-six miles, even done at a very slow pace, will take too much out of you in training. That's why most runners don't run more than a few marathons a year. After you've run one, you can't effectively handle another twenty-six miles for weeks or even months. However, if you've been training consistently and run about twenty miles a few times, you should be fit enough to extend your maximum distance on the day of the race. Also, you would have been holding back something in training, even for the twenty-milers, and for the actual marathon you won't hold back in terms of the overall effort. You'll probably have to extend yourself to the limit to be able to run the full twenty-six miles. A final factor is the emotional one. In training, a twenty-mile workout may, in the end, not be much "fun." However, the thrill of the marathon and the "support" of the exciting atmosphere will help you to run a greater distance.

SPECIAL NUTRITIONAL CONSIDERATIONS

There's more about food and drink in Chapter 8, but you should be reminded to take in added carbohydrates in the three days before the marathon, as "carbo-loading" has been proved to be an effective way to stock up on the fuel needed for the long miles. Eat an early dinner the night before the race and a light early breakfast, at least three hours before the start on race day. Some people stock up on carbos with pancakes on race morning, but to play it safe, go for a light meal, toast, cereal, coffee, nothing more involved than that. Make sure it is your habit to keep yourself hydrated in general to facilitate good training, and this extends to the premarathon period. In the hours before the race, depending on the weather, you'll want to drink at least twelve ounces of liquid, preferably water.

HOW TO RUN A MARATHON

By this point, having run several races, you're familiar with the many things, small and large, that go into the final race preparations. That indeed is one reason to be racing in the months prior to a first marathon; it helps you to feel comfortable and confident and organized when the marathon arrives. You know the ropes. Anyone who runs a marathon as his or her first race is making a terrible mistake.

The physiologists tell us that even pace, as we have advised for a 10K, is the best approach for the marathon, and this has been shown time and again. Go out easy. There's no hurry. Even the champions tend to go out easy. Run your pace; go with the flow. It's time, frankly, for clichés. It's time to "listen to your body" and run under control.

Sometimes sponges are available to rinse the body in a marathon. If they are, use them. But try not to let water drip into your socks and shoes.

At the Honolulu Marathon, the runners are treated to luscious scenery, which helps when you're faced with twenty-six miles. Here, runners head past Diamond Head as dawn breaks over the Pacific Ocean.

Take drinks when you need to. (Stop, and get the liquid down the hatch.) Check your mile times. Enjoy the scenery. Though stopping to drink can break your rhythm, it can also provide your body with a little relief; but, more than that, you must take in fluids to keep your system going. This is critical.

If you can control yourself physically and run the desired even pace, you've got half the battle won. The other half is mental. Here the psychologists take over. They have found that most marathoners achieve success by staying in tune with their precise body feelings for most of the race but not so much that they don't let their minds wander in a trancelike state to get through the difficult stages in the latter miles. A combined approach, it has been found, works best. Listen to your body so as to run at the best pace, but if, for whatever reason, the going gets tough, drift from the discomfort, instead of dwelling upon it, to break through the rough spots. Think of something else. Imagine yourself finishing and how good *that* will feel. Each runner (and every run) is different, so you have to be prepared to switch gears, depending on the circumstances. You have to be flexible in your mental gymnastics.

THE WALL

The wall is the somewhat mystical point in the last five or six miles of a marathon when your body's fuel is used up and an overwhelming fatigue sets in, making it tough to finish. Though the idea of the wall is simple, the reasons for coming upon it can be complex. You can be extremely well trained and still hit the wall. Biochemistry takes funny bounces. Some runners never hit the wall. Good for them. Chances are, you'll hit it in your first marathon, no matter what. The hope is that it will be benign. Be prepared to feel a little dazed and irritable and "wasted" with four or five miles to go. Your pace will slow, you may develop little aches and pains, you'll feel a little fed up and annoyed. Chances are, you'll get through it and manage to finish the race without much pain. You may have to walk a little in the last few miles, and that's O.K. People do it. At its worst, the wall will cause your leg muscles to cramp—the calves and hamstrings in particular—and that will feel awful. You'll have to stop and walk for a while and try to knead out the cramps. You may be reduced to a survival shuffle for the last few miles. Don't insist on finishing if you find yourself in deep trouble. It is simply not good for your health to finish at all cost. People do drop out if necessary. Even the champions drop out.

THE FINISH

If you've made it—and if you've trained sensibly and run the marathon intelligently, I think you will—enjoy it. Don't dwell on your time, whatever it is. You've finished. As much as you may be hurting, you should also feel great. You made your goal. You ran a marathon. You succeeded in taking on the challenge and running the twenty-six miles 385 yards.

Once you've gotten a grip on yourself, do a little light stretching

The feeling of finishing can be one of elation, whether you're a champion, like Toshihiko Seko of Japan...

(nothing severe) and take a crack at a little jogging. If that's too discomforting, a good walk will do. Drink a lot, and when you're up to it, eat a lot. Put an ice pack to any localized soreness. Then take a warm bath. Then go to sleep.

...or part of the middle of the pack at New York.

RECOVERY

The next day, you'll feel worse. That's part of the game. You'll feel so stiff you won't be able to walk downstairs normally. It'll take from a few days to a week to get rid of the soreness, more if you really hit the wall and suffered. The length of recovery is directly related to the degree of difficulty you experienced in the race. Bad cases are known to take months to get over the shock of a marathon. That's part of the risk.

Studies have found that recovery time and ease are not affected by any light running you may do in the week following the marathon. Most runners, however, like to jog a little just to keep active. In a week you should be able to run a comfortable five miles again. You'll need to eat after the marathon as you did before it: carbo-loading to recovery. The race will have depleted your energy supply and you'll need to fill up again.

YOUR NEXT MARATHON

Many runners experience postmarathon blues. After months of living with the daily challenge of an ambitious training program, the challenge has finally come and gone and ... now you're left wondering what comes next. There's "nothing to do." There's no aim. There's no mission to drive you. You'll wonder how much running you should continue to do.

I say don't feel sorry for yourself. Get rid of postmarathon blues by

---

MARATHON TRAINING CHART

Stage I (see Chapter 9)

In review: gradual development to a training load of 45 miles a week, with a long run of 10 miles.

Stage II

	Weekly Mileage	Longest Run
Month 1	45	12 miles
Month 2	50	14 miles
Month 3	50	16 miles

Stage III

Month 4	55	18 miles
Month 5	55	20 miles
Month 6	60	20 miles

deciding right then and there that you're not going to run another marathon for a while, that you're going to allow for the natural healing process of recovery to take place, and then, if you feel you need a new goal, a new challenge, you'll consider working on your speed (instead of distance) and focusing on shorter events that take less out of you but are in no way less of a challenge.

In a way, the shorter races are harder. For most people it's easier to run long and slow than short and fast. So, forget about the marathon for a time. For a month, don't even think about running another one. And then, if you decide to take the plunge again (this time, no doubt, shooting for a better time), remember how it felt in your first one with a few miles to go, and then perhaps you'll wise up and reconsider.

11

Special Running Considerations

CHILDREN

Watching kids run is one of life's pleasures. They look like miniatures of top runners. They get their knees up high and their chins out and they work their arms and bounce along, full of spirit and energy. They don't particularly think about it. They just do it. This spontaneity is a wonderful thing, but as the running movement has grown, kids have begun to imitate their moms and dads and older brothers and sisters, and gotten "into it." Boys and girls of six or seven or ten are running in a structured manner, training and competing, even over long distances. So much so that people in the sport have begun to take sides over how much is too much where kids are concerned. Kids are people too, and if running is good for older folks running is good for . . . everyone. But kids are also young and vulnerable, and subject to the sometimes foolish ideas of us adults, who have the responsibility of setting them on the right path.

So the question exists, What kind of running is best for kids so that they can benefit from it in both the short term and the long?

The answers are hard to come by. In the first place, the same question is asked of adults as well, and we don't have all the answers for ourselves, either. Many of us wish to develop our running to its fullest potential, and in trying to do so fear that we may, at times, overdo it. That fear of overdoing it is primarily what has made the matter of children and running into an issue. If young people run too much at an early age, it could harm them physically and emotionally, perhaps irreparably.

Not everyone believes that, however. There are those who say children are not so brittle and can pretty much run any which way they want—or any which way we tell them they should—and they'll do just fine. The right course probably lies somewhere in between. I've gone through the experience intimately, because my own children run, and I'm still not sure exactly what's best for them. And as I watch over my kids' running, I find I still have much to learn.

Kids can start running at an early age as long as they're allowed to do it freely, without parental pressure for overachievement. *(Steve Sutton/DUOMO)*

We have two girls, Jamie, six, and Allison, twelve. Jamie doesn't do any formal running yet. Occasionally, on a family outing to the track for a workout, she'll run a few laps. She seems to have boundless energy, inspired by the example of her older sister and myself and my wife. Jamie probably runs upward of a mile in the course of a typical day of play, and she well may soon enter age-group competition and start to "jog" with regularity, as Allison started to do at about her age.

Once Jamie starts to compete—purely for the fun of it—it will be both easier and harder for her than it was for Allison at the beginning. Easier because she'll feel at home in the sport, having been a part of it already and watched her sister compete for years. Harder because she'll have her sister's success to live up to, no matter how much we try to deny that. One thing I know I'm going to do is coax Jamie into different events from those Allison has run. It's a good idea to have kids run many different events anyway, but Allison seems to have found a home in the half-mile (or eight hundred meters), though she's also run the mile, the two-mile and a couple of road races of five miles and ten thousand meters. Jamie, being a different body type and personality, might be better off at first in the sprints. It just might feel right to her, and it'll give her a chance to establish her own running identity within the family.

But should kids compete at all? Let them decide. Encouragement is one thing, parental pressure quite another. A kid may be competitive by nature, wish to compete and thrive on it. Another kid may feel he has all the competition he needs in school or in other environments and doesn't need the added burdens of running competition. Such a child may not be able to articulate that feeling; you'll have to be smart enough to sense it. In many cases it will be triumph enough that the child enjoys running and wants to do it, without the added element of competition.

Competition is a very risky thing for anyone, especially kids. We adults, perhaps, can better understand the complexities of competition and deal rationally with success and failure. What do we do when a kid who enjoys running decides, after "losing" a race, that he doesn't want to run any more? I've seen high school athletes quit when things didn't go their way. (I've also seen high school kids who were remarkably successful ultimately "burn out" and quit—before they could enjoy running as adults.)

In my view, the best sort of running environment for a child is one that includes his peers—perhaps a running club (or "team") that will serve as a support system for running, have social benefits as well and, with the right sort of balance and emphasis, keep competition (if there is any) in perspective so that a child will learn how to win, how to "lose," and how to try hard. This type of environment would have enough goals and direction to build discipline and character, but not so much that the program loses sight of the primary objectives of the running activity: to promote good health, a love of sport, an appreciation of excellence and a camaraderie and sharing among friends. In other words, running can be the activity, like any activity, that helps to develop positive growth in a child.

Unfortunately, from what I've seen, there is all too little of this sort of group running, especially for girls, until you get into the formal high school sports program. And so with Allison I had to be the encouraging

Kids can benefit from competition and usually adapt well to training, once they've had sufficient running experience.

force, and while she matured into it, running was a source of both fun and friction within the family.

Most of it surely was enjoyable, but I know there were times when Allison resented her running, because it took her away from her friends (who were not runners) or forced her to choose between one and the other, creating guilt no matter what the choice. I don't know if we'd do it any differently, had we to do it over again with Allison. We had her running a few times a week when she was six, seven and eight, never more than a couple of miles at a time. She did this with no trouble; physically, she felt good running, but too often what running represented to her seemed to get in the way—it made her "different" and she found this hard to accept.

Allison was competing then too. By getting her fit and offering to take her to events, we provided the opportunity. The decision was hers. In time, she responded well to the competition, and we hoped, more than anything, that the entire running experience would serve to make her more independent so she would not take up with the wrong crowd as a teenager, give her something constructive to do so she wouldn't have time to waste, and provide an athletic outlet for her—something challenging in which she might succeed.

I've seen six-year-olds compete with more poise than do adults—I guess some of them don't know any better. Allison did. Being in a family in which running is talked about a lot and is, in fact, a big part of Daddy's work, Allison perhaps knew too much. She was too ready to evaluate her various racing performances, unlike other kids, who had no idea what their times meant, only that they'd placed first or third or sixth in the race. We've had to steer Allison away from imitating Mommy or Daddy and worrying about her times, and encourage her simply to respond to the competition, without concern for the stopwatch.

One way in which we accomplished this was to enter Allison in longer-distance open road races. In these events, finishing was enough of a reward, and since Allison would finish ahead of many adults and most (or all) of the kids her age, her self-esteem, no matter what her "performance," could remain high. Also, because there'd be few kids her age in the race and these kids would be spread out in a field of hundreds or thousands of runners, Allison would be competing against herself, not the other kids—as she would do in the highly competitive indoor track meets she'd run in winter. So this form of noncompetitive racing, though less of a challenge, balanced

Kids should know they can stop in a race if necessary; otherwise they could overdo it.

out the more structured events and provided less risk of failure and more safety for the ego.

In fact, in the more relaxed atmosphere Allison would sometimes run better, not fearful of failure. The indoor track events were certainly harder: the competition was keen and intense, and no matter how you tried to de-emphasize it, risky. When Allison went to the starting line in an eight-hundred-meter race against other girls her age, there was no hiding in the pack. These races were short and fast, and your instincts were clearly exposed. Every kid was timed, and afterward there could be no secret as to how well you'd done. You knew your place and time and everyone else's.

I knew the risks. I had done it as a youth. Your stomach churns beforehand, and afterward you're thrilled that it's over. It's a hard thing to do, let alone to do well, but I think kids can benefit from it, as long as it's just one element in a total running (or sports) program. When I see kids compete like that year-round, it worries me.

Allison spends about two months preparing for and participating in these indoor track meets. It's her annual project. At all other times her running is far less structured and demanding. At times, as over the summer, she hardly runs at all. We have only one basic rule: if she wants to compete, she has to be prepared. That means she will have had to train sufficiently to be prepared. We feel that's analogous to other things, such as school. If you want to do well on a test, you have to study. Same with running. If you want to compete, you have to be ready for it.

It was Allison, following my wife's example, who decided to run in the L'eggs Mini-Marathon, a highly popular women's ten-kilometer race held in New York's Central Park every spring. To be physically capable of running 6.2 miles, we made sure Allison ran her usual four times a week for a couple of months, with a long run of 4-5 miles once a week. She was ten, and she ran it well, completing the distance comfortably. She felt fine afterward and was evidently thrilled to have done it. She was one of the youngest in the field of over five thousand.

The youngest kid was eight, and it was this little girl who was the first child to finish. I knew who this kid was, because she had an armful of age-group records to her credit. I'd heard she regularly ran forty or fifty miles a week and that she'd run a few marathons. She seemed no worse for the wear, but frankly, I disapprove of that. We know too little about the athletic development of kids, physically and emotionally, to allow them to run something like a marathon. I can't believe that it can be in an eight-year-old's best interests to run twenty-six miles, no matter how well trained she might be. Most medical authorities agree that such ambitious running is potentially harmful to kids.

Of course, there are those who would question what we've done with Allison. By age eleven she'd been running and competing for five years, had run as long as six miles at once, and had made a commitment to running. Who knows what that would signify to her as she got older? We're working on it with her, helping her to grow as an athlete and a human being. Perhaps the two are not so different.

SENIOR CITIZENS

By now the story of the person who discovered running in the twilight of his years and emerged as a vigorous and healthier elder with a zest for life is quite well known. We are all familiar with someone in his sixties or seventies who runs regularly and feels great, perhaps competes, and is committed to the running lifestyle. Though such examples are now clichés, there is a profound lesson for all of us in the experience of these senior citizens. They have proved, beyond a doubt, that running works, that it can be made to work; they answer all of the doubts of people who know running is good for them but have yet to do it because they wonder, Am I too old? too heavy? too sedentary for too long? too set in my ways? too busy? too fearful of exercise? too this, or too that? If people who had never run a day in their lives, grandmothers and grandfathers, people perhaps not in the best of health once, have learned to run and enjoy it and have become better off for it, then we must be convinced of running's unique properties and the opportunities it offers to everyone.

End of lecture. The images the uninitiated have of these people is of feeble old men or women shuffling around at a snail's pace—at a fast walk—accomplishing what? they wonder. First, the image is wrong. Many of these people have become athletes. Those who are not after sport, who are content to jog, are doing themselves the same world of good as younger folks who jog for basic health benefits. With their doctors' blessing (a physical checkup for "clearance" is necessary for most older people, especially those who have been sedentary), they have become active, keeping their bodies moving as they are meant to be, for upward of thirty or forty or sixty minutes a day three or four times a week. They've lowered their pulse and blood pressure, they've strengthened their heart, developed some muscle tone, lost weight, acquired defenses against the diseases of aging, and have a better outlook on life.

But back to the athletes. These older sportsmen and -women are causing us to redefine what it means to age. They have expanded our notions of what we can accomplish as we get older. We see them at events competing in what is known as the "masters" division, for runners forty and older. They are thin, strong, fit and fast. They train.

The masters sports movement is growing throughout the world, with running and track and field among its most popular segments. The U.S.

People can run at any age, and for runners forty and over there are thriving "masters" competitions in track and road racing.

road-running boom, with its accessibility to every sector of our population, has contributed to this. Virtually every race has a masters division in which places are scored and awards given in age groups to men and women forty and older.

Older runners are subject to much the same stresses of running as their younger counterparts. Though muscle mass and oxygen uptake potential decline with age, beginning at around age thirty-five, runners in their forties, fifties, sixties, seventies need not worry that they might be incapable of running with regularity and with occasional intensity.

The one tendency of older athletes that sports scientists feel they have determined is that, once in your thirties, you will start to recover more slowly from injury.

Now, in my late thirties, I can attest to that. Though my running is more conservative these days, I still seem to incur injury; and when I do get hurt it also seems to take longer for me to fully recover. One apparent reason for this is an increasing reduction in flexibility with age. A lack of flexibility is sometimes associated with prevalence of injury.

Older women can perform well too. This is Cindy Dalrymple, one of the leading forty-and-over-women runners in the United States.

The best example of the benefits of exercise for total health and fulfillment: Ol' Johnny Kelley, who still runs the Boston Marathon at age 77. He's run Boston 54 times. Recent tests showed Kelley to be fitter than most 40-year-olds. *(Janeart)*

It is appropriate that one of our greatest evangelists on behalf of running is a man in his sixties, a physician, the best-selling author, lecturer and philosopher George Sheehan. Now sixty-six (retirement age, he would laugh), Dr. Sheehan has for years been entertaining and inspiring legions of runners by debunking medical myths about exercise, age and opportunity and, in a sense, defining a new age of fitness in which we all have the chance to reach a newfound potential.

Sheehan practices what he preaches, by competing almost every weekend in races around the country. In his writings and his talks, he has expressed the drive to compete and the meaning of the *race,* and I have seen it in Sheehan close up, because we are "neighbors" in Monmouth County, New Jersey, about an hour's drive south of New York City. Frequently we find each other at the same local races, and when George is running I know I'll have to be fit and push hard to keep up with him. It has to be pretty cool for him to run with a shirt, and when he's shirtless you can see he's not boasting when he says he weighs the same 130 pounds he weighed as a varsity runner in college almost a half century ago.

The examples of this sort of spirited running among older folks are endless. I'll use two more. Marian Epstein and her husband, Irving, of Brooklyn, New York, are both sixty-seven. I've known them for years and have written about them before. They've been running since 1970, and they race regularly and frequently side by side, and their enthusiasm has not dimmed even though they usually finish last. They are a charming couple with a reputation throughout the New York area, and people love them not because it's cute to see old folks jog in last, but

A good women's example is, at right, Sister Marion Irvine, a nun, who at the age of 54 ran a 2:51 marathon and became the oldest qualifier for the 1984 Olympic Trials in the marathon. *(Kenneth Lee)*

Older runners must abide by the same rules of running as their young counterparts.

because the Epsteins have succeeded as committed runners, indeed as athletes. They run marathons. It may take them five hours, but they do it and enjoy it. They persevere. Marian was ill before she ran. She hasn't been ill since. (Another Marion, by the way, Sister Marion Irvine, a nun from California, ran a Z:51 marathon at age fifty-four and qualified for the 1984 women's Olympic Trial in the marathon.)

"To me," says Marian Epstein, "running a marathon is like living. It helps me mentally and physically. It's so special because I know I can conquer it. It makes me feel beautiful. I just can't describe it any other way. It's a challenge. Just to be there and know I can do it."

The, other example is Hal Higdon, of Michigan City, Indiana. To runners, Hal, a senior writer for *The Runner,* needs no introduction. As journalist and athlete, he is one of America's leading forces in running, perhaps as influential as even George Sheehan. In 1964, at thirty-two, he placed fourth in the Boston Marathon, the first American to finish that year. Today, at fifty-three, Hal is a leading masters runner, and his marathon time, at his best, has slowed by only about ten minutes in twenty years. He has grown children who run, and one of them, Kevin, qualified to run in the 1984 Olympic Marathon Trial. Still, Kevin has to be pretty fit to beat his dad. Hal has been a subject in a longevity study and has been found to have lost only small percentages of fitness over the past two decades, owing primarily to his consistent and substantial exercise over the course of his entire adult life. I suspect that twenty years from now, when Hal is seventy-three, he will be just as fit, if not as fast.

But, by then, there'll be a lot of competition in the seventy-and-over age group.

WOMEN

Opportunity

Women's running has been nothing short of revolutionary, a result of the growth in women's sports in general, which was fueled, no doubt, by the women's movement in all aspects of life. Was it really as recently as 1972 that women were denied entry into the New York Marathon? Yes, and how ironic it is that the New York Marathon, in particular, through the remarkable performances of Norway's Grete Waitz, has sparked extraordinary interest in the ability of women to run.

Most polls indicate that women now make up about 25 percent of the total U.S. running population, and this percentage extends to competition, in which women's participation has been growing. Now that there is finally an Olympic marathon for women there is virtually no opportunity in running that is not as available to women as to men. Most high schools and colleges have track and cross-country teams and championship events for women as well as men. Women can compete in any road race they wish, and the prize structure usually is equal for both sexes, or at least proportionately equal based on the numbers of participants. Women have national racing circuits all their own—those sponsored by Avon, L'eggs, Bonne Bell and Moving Comfort. Avon's international marathon (held in Paris in 1984) is world famous, as are the major ten-kilometer events promoted by L'eggs in New York and Bonne Bell in Boston.

Another major program, now in its eleventh year, is the Colgate Women's Games, in New York, a series of indoor track meets open to

Women are no less competitive than men, once they gain experience in running. *(Janeart)*

girls and women of all ages. Girls as young as five or six can compete free in qualifying rounds that lead to a final, televised meet in Madison Square Garden. As many as twenty thousand contestants from New York and a number of surrounding counties have taken part in the program in a single year, many winning scholarship grants and developing into champions in the high school and college ranks.

Need

From what I've observed, and what studies are starting to indicate, it may be said that women "need" running more than men. Running, as

There are numerous women's races providing important opportunities for women, such as the programs put on by Avon and Bonne Bell.

we have stated, offers the chance to strive for something, to fulfill goals, to make progress and succeed in many ways; and women, even in the 1990s, generally have less of a chance for those things than do men. Consequently, we are seeing many otherwise unfulfilled women embrace running as something very critical to their emotional well-being, not to mention the physical.

Those women who run who are without stimulating careers latch onto running as an essential outlet for physical activity, their one chance "to do something for myself" in the course of a family-oriented day. I've certainly seen this in my wife, Andrea, who stopped her school teaching for a number of years when the children came. She talked about her need for running as a guest on "Good Morning, America," which asked her on as a first-time marathoner before the New York Marathon one year. As Andrea explained, her hour of running a day is hers and hers alone, not something she has to do for the kids or me or "the family."

Conflict

However, surveys have indicated that running can be a source of division and conflict in a relationship, and even responsible for divorce. In fact, the divorce rate among couples in which one mate runs seriously has been found to be much higher than that of the general population. One typical situation is the nonrunning, nonathletic husband who can't cope with a running wife—a successful one who is perhaps as devoted to her sport as she is to the family. Once, I had a long talk with a young woman I know who could be described as a very serious runner. She and her husband had just split up over her running. According to her, he just couldn't accept her athletic ambitions.

Still, there are numerous examples of relationships that have been strengthened by running. I might suggest that my own marriage has been one such relationship. Before my wife began running, my running was too often a source of conflict. I ran too much, my wife couldn't understand it, and there were times when she wanted us to do something but we couldn't because I had to run. When she took up running, it was one more thing we could share, and I adapted my own schedule so she could run. It's worked out, and whenever possible we run together. When we race, which isn't that often, we'll pick a race that suits us both. I think I've been supportive and helped her to get more out of her running. Now she's more compulsive about it than I am.

Potential

The primary difference in the physiology of men and women is that women tend to have less muscle mass, and since muscle is required to "work," women will tend to have performances inferior to those of men, all other things being equal. The world records for women are roughly 10 percent slower than those for men (e.g., 2:07:11 vs. 2:21:06 in the marathon; 9:93 vs. 10:76 in the hundred meters).

However, among average runners it seems there is no difference and that performance will be based primarily on effort and determination. We middle-of-the-pack men have all seen our egos bruised by women our age leaving us in the dust.

Women also tend to have more fat than men, and at one time this was thought to aid them in marathon running because of the low incidence of women "hitting the wall." The latest thinking on that, however, is that greater fat-burning capacity is not at work here; instead, it is thought that women, new to competition, had been unaccustomed to going all out and therefore less likely to crash by running "over their heads" in a marathon.

Training

Women can train just as men train. They can run long, they can run fast, they can run twice a day, they can do whatever they want. And the training effect will be the same: they will improve and become better runners. The only thing they can't do is run speed work as fast as men, because, again, reduced muscle mass will keep them a few steps behind. But the relative intensity can be the same. Women, we are also finding, can overdo it as foolishly as men.

Injury

Overdoing it can lead to injury, of course. The pattern of injury to women differs somewhat from that to men. For example, the curvature in the pelvic area can cause a crossover in the running stride, and this

It was not until the early 1970s that women were allowed to compete in Marathons. In 1978 Grete Waitz entered her first Marathon and broke the women's world record.

can produce a greater incidence of certain types of leg injuries, including stress fractures in the pelvic area itself. Because of this tendency, certain women also can be predisposed to runner's knee, because there results an irritation to the cartilage. Such cases can be treated like other knee injuries where foot inserts are used to balance the foot strike and limit leg rotation.

Pregnancy

The growth of women's running has given birth to a field known as sports gynecology, which studies how exercise affects reproductive functioning. One of the field's biggest concerns is the pregnant runner, and most authorities agree that running during the early months of pregnancy is not only acceptable but advisable, because women who are physically fit seem to tolerate the workload of labor and delivery better than the unfit. Women should not *begin* a running program during pregnancy, but women who ran before pregnancy, in most cases, could continue for some months with no ill effects on themselves or their children. Women should always proceed under the advice of their doctors; in some cases, running will be prohibited, possibly because the doctor is not that familiar with running or sports medicine, or he is simply con-

Two leading women, Allison Roe (left) and Patti Catalano, show they run just as well as leading male runners, at the Boston Marathon. Still, the men's world record is 14 minutes faster than the women's. *(Paul Sutton/DUOMO)*

servative in his approach, or there is something about you or your pregnancy that warrants caution.

Amenorrhea

A number of surveys of women runners has shown that such athletes have a higher incidence of menstrual irregularity than nonathletes, but since so many factors can produce this irregularity it's hard to pin it on running alone. Exercise alone may not be at fault. Still, the pattern seems to exist, and further study may reveal whether it is the running that causes this. There are many serious runners—including at least one group of top-level college athletes that I'm aware of—that have not had their periods in years.

Anorexia nervosa

This complicated illness, associated with young women runners and others, results in a compulsive need to look and feel thin, producing self-inflicted starvation and, in its extreme, death. This is an oversimplification of a disease that is not yet fully understood. It is important for parents, coaches and others who supervise young women runners to watch for any signs of incipient anorexia, such as forced vomiting and an excessive, "bag of bones," thinness, beyond the purely athletic benefits of low body fat.

Perhaps the greatest universal benefit of running is that it is not, like other sports, restricted to the naturally athletic. It is truly for everyone, and for that our whole society can be thankful.

12

A Program for the Advanced Runner

Who is the advanced runner? He, or she, is the runner in the front row of a racing field primed to knock out a fast five miles, the speaker at the prerace clinic giving advice on training and competition, the person next door who runs six marathons a year, the varsity athlete still running after college, the young runner breaking age-group records, the retired cop running sixty-five miles a week.

There are countless types of advanced runners, just as there is no one type of "average" runner. There are two primary traits, however, that all advanced runners have in common: commitment and ability. Some have one or the other; most have both. That is what separates the average runner from the more advanced runner. It is fairly common to find runners of great commitment but limited ability. These are serious runners who train substantially, compete regularly and hunger for better performance. They run well, but you'll never find them winning a race, or even winning their age group. They're struggling to shave a few minutes from their marathon time.

On the other hand, there are few runners of great ability and little commitment. A runner who has a talent would have had to run seriously to uncover it. And this discovery would probably spur him on. There are not many people around wasting their running talent (except at the high school level, where coaches will complain about students with potential who are not developing it). Adults who struggle with their running would give anything for the sort of natural ability evident in young runners. Some adults have it; it's a gift, something to cherish and mold.

How can you tell if you're an advanced runner? That's like asking the price of a precious jewel. If you have to ask, you can't afford it. If you're an advanced runner, you know it. If you're not sure, you're not (yet) one of them.

The question to ask is, Could I become one and if so, would I want to? The first part relates to ability, the second to commitment. Commitment is the easier quality to develop. If you truly enjoy running, if you thrive on achievement, if performance is meaningful to you, if your lifestyle allows for a dedication to running in terms of time and energy— then you can make the commitment. Many runners do it. Far beyond achieving a healthy state by running, people run as a way of life, as a vehicle to achieve. Their commitment is strong. That's the "easy" part.

Alberto Salazar shows the smooth form common to the better runners, even in a marathon.

See the aggressiveness displayed in competition between Jon Sinclair and Herb Lindsay. Motivation plays a big part in running performance.

But your commitment can take you only so far. Ability in running, like ability in many other sports, is genetic. But it can be developed— and that's one reason running is so popular. People who considered themselves unathletic, who never played for their high school teams, who couldn't sink a twenty-foot jump shot if their life depended on it, can train to run a marathon. Imagine that. But completing the distance is one thing; running it fast, in a certain time, is quite another. That's where ability comes in.

I remember a line from the award-winning film *Chariots of Fire.* Sam Mussabini, the sprint coach, tells his prospective pupil Harold Abrahams, who would win the hundred meters in the 1924 Olympics, "I can't put in what God left out." He was smart. He could not make Abrahams any *faster.* He *could* help him with technique and fundamentals to enable Abrahams to reach his potential. That's what a good coach does. Ability and desire take care of the rest.

Most of us are self-coached, and so it is our job, if we care to, to determine where our strengths and weaknesses lie, to explore our limits, to maximize whatever God gave us. Sometimes it is hard to determine exactly what it is that we were given, so here are some attributes common to advanced runners.

1. Oxygen use. The rate at which we take in oxygen and transport it through the body is called maximum oxygen uptake, or VO2 max, as the exercise physiologists term it. The better runners have a high rate of

Better runners, when tested for oxygen "uptake," show a high capacity for utilizing oxygen.

oxygen use, and when tested on a treadmill run, usually "score" in the high seventies or even eighties in terms of milliliters of oxygen used per minute. By comparison, when I was tested once I scored fifty-nine. Oxygen use can increase through training, but only up to a point.

2. Biomechanics. The more efficiently you run, the better use you make of your energy sources, such as the oxygen you take in. What is efficient running? It varies from one runner to the next, but a smooth, fluid stride and little wasted motion are among the characteristics associated with efficient running.

Most runners probably think they run more efficiently than they do. You can't always feel your faults—you need someone to point them out, or, if possible, a video to be made of your running (a service some running stores are now providing for their customers). It's like hearing your voice on tape—you'll be surprised, and perhaps a little disappointed.

Stride length is something you might be able to determine even if you can't measure it. The average runner likely has a short, "shuffling" stride in which the feet slam the ground heel first and the knees barely lift. The advanced runner, because of better body mechanics, likely has a longer stride, in which the foot strike is not solely heel first and the knees lift. This is an oversimplification, but the point is, there's a way to run fast, and this way is not natural to many runners.

3. Muscle fiber. This is something else that can be determined with certainty only with laboratory testing. A muscle biopsy of the leg tissue will reveal the percentage of slow-twitch and fast-twitch muscle fiber. Advanced distance runners tend to have a majority of slow-twitch fiber; sprinters and middle-distance runners have more fast-twitch. With a high percentage of slow-twitch fiber, you would be better able to recruit the muscle energy necessary to run for long distances at a slow pace. The fast-twitch fiber makes possible the powerful bursts of speed that sprinters must be capable of.

Instinctively, however, you can probably take a good guess at your predispositions. If you've been running long enough, and especially if you keep accurate records of your running (say, in diary form—which I don't, by the way), you can try to determine whether you're more naturally suited to the sort of twenty-mile training runs advised for marathon training, or shorter forms of intense running, such as speed work or short races. There are probably many runners who have realized they're more naturally suited to hard, fast running but who run greater dis-

African runners such as Kenya's Michael Musyoki are excellently conditioned, because of their upbringing in a high-altitude environment.

tances at slow speeds because marathon goals dance in their heads, or because it's less complicated to go out and run at an easy pace for ten miles than to construct a logical speed workout.

4. Body type. Let's face it: fat people don't make good runners. For distance running, the thinner you are the better off you are, up to a point. Most advanced male runners have less than 10 percent body fat (about half that of the average sedentary male). Their female counterparts usually have less than 15 percent—in general women commonly have at least 25 percent body fat.

A rule of thumb used to determine the appropriate weight for optimal competitive running is this: your weight should be double your height in inches. If you're six feet tall (72 inches), you should weigh about 144. If you're 5'8" (68 inches), you should weigh 136. Of course

Joan Samuelson set new standards for top women runners by breaking the world marathon record by over two minutes at Boston in 1983. *(Jeff Johnson)*

this varies with body type, but remember, the ectomorph—the narrow, skinny, small-boned "weakling" we used to make fun of in high school gym class—is today's top distance runner. Bill Rodgers is 5'8" and weighs 128. Frank Shorter is 5'10" and weighs 130. Even my running buddy Jimmy is built that way. Like me, he's 5'9", but unlike me he weighs 135. I weigh 155. Need I say more?

5. Injury. Here the advanced runner shows two patterns. First, he or she rarely gets injured, or certainly less so than the rest of us. And when he does, he recovers more easily and regains fitness more readily as well. To use an extreme example, Eamonn Coghlan, the Irish Olympian, missed much of the 1982 season with serious injuries. He did no running at all for months. In the winter of '83 he broke the world indoor mile record, and in the summer of '83 he won the world title in the 5,000 meters. Allow me to use my friend Jimmy again. As I've stated (Chapter six), he never gets injured. Therefore, he's always fit, always ready to perform in races, never out of shape—though sometimes, from all his running, he'll admit to feeling "stale." Me—I'm injured half the time. It's my nature. That means I spend a good deal of time recovering from injury and getting in shape again. You can't run too many quality races or hope to reach your potential if you're like me.

6. Postrace recovery. The better runners race a 10K, and afterward they run another six miles to get in their mileage, and the next day they run ten miles as though nothing happened. This is a sign that you have something special going for you. Going all out in competition happens not to tear you down. The average runner is different after a race. He has aches and irritations. He's stiff. He wants to nap. He can't run normally for a few days. He's cranky. And we're not even talking about a marathon. The body's message is undeniable.

7. Body feelings. Speaking of the body's message, serious average runners will find their bodies talking to them at odd hours. Fatigue, ache, pain, strain, funny noises and such are not what you want to experience in the course of the day from your feet, knees, muscles and even upper body. The typical runner running every day and racing will feel and hear things like this; this is the body's way of telling you to take it easy, or to see a doctor. Advanced runners don't experience this constant telegraphing of trouble. Theirs is more irregular, and usually they have to do something stupid to bring it on. The rest of us simply experience it because that's the way we are.

Notice the clean, upright running form of Bill Rodgers, even as he grows tired in a marathon.

8. Motivation. Mental toughness is very important in running. It's what distinguishes the top runners as well. And if you don't have much of it, you can't go very far with your running. It's an intangible quality. It has to do with drive and determination, how badly you really want something and, at times, how much of yourself you're willing to give to get it.

As a borderline advanced runner (in the loosest definition of the term), I don't score well in this category. The few races I've been satisfied with, I can look back on and realize I ran mentally tough. Most times I don't.

Four of the world's best runners show the intensity of competition: from left, Rod Dixon (New Zealand), Robert de Castella (Australia), Craig Virgin (U.S.) and Michael Musyoki (Kenya).

In one five-mile race, I ran along with my pal Evan. We've been dear friends since childhood. Evan has always been a good athlete (and now he is a terrific college basketball coach). No one has ever tried harder than Evan. Running, however, was never his best sport as a kid, but he would become a runner, a pretty good one, and for this five-miler he was in excellent shape. I was not—that's why I planned simply to run with Evan. We ran together for four and a half miles. Then Evan pulled away from me. I was tired. So was he. I had far more basic speed than he. He was tougher. He wanted to kick it in. I know I could have run in to the finish with him, but something inside me gave in to the late-race discomfort I was feeling, and that was that. He finished about five seconds ahead of me.

9. Time. The time you have to train will affect your time in a race. Advanced runners need ample time to train. There's no two ways about it. How are you going to get fit enough to perform well if you can squeeze in only a little time here and there because of work obligations, family responsibility or other interests? The better runners sometimes train twice a day—the champions certainly do.

Still, it depends how you make use of your time. If you have a lot of time but just go through the motions, you're not really training, not the way you have to in order to reach your potential. Your *time* devoted to training must include time spent thinking about running, planning your workouts, evaluating them, perhaps conferring with a coach if you're lucky enough to have one. You need the time to focus on your running; that's part of the commitment. If the desire is there but not the time, realize that, and also that unless it is, you'll be unable to become an "advanced" runner.

HOW THE ADVANCED
RUNNER SHOULD TRAIN

Because runners at every level differ so, one training program does not fit all. However, as we have stated, the principles of sensible training, by and large, remain the same. And so hypothetical training programs are always flexible, elastic, even shapeless. They are merely guidelines. You take parts of them and adapt them to your needs, goals, conditions, interests. Before getting down the specifics, let's look at some of the principles for the advanced runner, or a person hoping to become one. Advanced runners should:

   1. run six days a week (sometimes seven);
   2. race at least once a month;
   3. try to peak twice a year (usually spring or fall, unless you run track—then you'll probably want to peak winter and summer);
   4. run at least 45 miles a week (60 a week for marathoners);
   5. run hard at least once a week (not counting a race);
   6. have access to sports-medicine specialists for periodic testing, massage therapy, injury diagnosis, and correction of bad running habits;
   7. do some track running;

8. run, on occasion, with a team, for the benefit of group support and some form of coaching;

9. utilize other forms of fitness training (e.g., swimming, biking) for supplemental exercise and for conditioning during periods of injury.

Specific Training

Here are sample weekly programs for three phases of training: building a foundation, getting stronger, getting sharper and racing-fit.

Building a Foundation: Typical Week

MONDAY: 10 miles average pace; swimming.

TUESDAY: 2-mile jog; 6-mile fartlek (unstructured varied pace) on soft terrain (trail or golf course); 2-mile jog.

WEDNESDAY: 12 miles average pace; weight work.

THURSDAY: 8 miles hard.

Track running is common to the advanced runner's training program.
(Steve Sutton/DUOMO)

FRIDAY: no running or 6-mile jog; weight work.
SATURDAY: 10 miles hard.
SUNDAY: 14-18 miles average pace.
TOTAL MILEAGE: 64—74 miles.

Getting Stronger: Typical Week

MONDAY: jog 1 mile; five 1½-mile loops with each loop progressively faster (start with average pace and end with 3-mile-race pace); jog 1 mile; swim.

TUESDAY: 2-mile jog; 5-mile fartlek on soft terrain; 2-mile jog.

Frank Shorter recommends interval running on a track —repeated runs of 1 or 2 or 3 laps with short rests in between—for optimal success. *(Gale Constable/DUOMO)*

WEDNESDAY: 10 miles average pace; weight work.

THURSDAY: jog 3 miles; 2 miles of striding the straightaways at good effort and jogging turns, at a track; jog 3 miles.

FRIDAY: no running, or jog 5 miles; weight work.

SATURDAY: 10 miles hard.

SUNDAY: 12-16 miles average pace.

TOTAL RUNNING: 59—68 miles.

Top women run-
ners such as Mary
Slaney train as hard
as men do, though
Slaney finds high
mileage does not
suit her. *(Paul Sut-
lun/DUOMO)*

Getting Sharper and Racing-Fit: Typical Week

MONDAY: jog 1 mile; five l-mile loops with each loop progressively faster (start with half-marathon pace and finish with 3-mile-race pace); jog 1 mile; swim.

TUESDAY: 2-mile jog; 4-mile fartlek on soft terrain; 2-mile jog.

WEDNESDAY: 8 miles average pace; weight work.

THURSDAY: jog 2 miles; eight 1/2-mile loops at 5-mile-race pace, with 220-yard jog recoveries; jog 2 miles.

FRIDAY: no running or jog 4 miles; weight work.

SATURDAY: 8 miles hard.

SUNDAY: 10-14 miles average pace.

TOTAL RUNNING: 50—58 miles.

Notice how Slaney is running in control, as opposed to her tired opponents, who are not as smooth.

Experienced competitors train to develop a kick so they can respond with good speed at the end of a race. *(Gale Constable/ DUOMO)*

These three phases might compose a given six-month period. The foundation period might last three months, the second phase two months and the peaking phase one month. When the peaking phase is over (you'll know when it is; you'll start to lose your zip, and signs of staleness will set in), let up, run relaxed for a while, then start the six-month cycle again.

Afterword

After years of focusing on short-term goals, experienced runners usually begin to feel a reduced immediacy to their fitness aims. They grow less concerned about the next year's marathon or the next week's race, and devote more thought and planning to long-term goals—that is, to a lifetime of good health and fitness. They structure their running accordingly.

They might run a little less and try to minimize the risk of injury. They might choose their races with greater care. They might add other forms of exercise to their fitness programs, to acquire a more well-rounded conditioning effect. Or they might continue to run as they have for years— thirty or fifty or seventy-five miles a week —but perhaps with a more flexible approach and with less emotional dependency on running in a tightly prescribed manner.

In time, most runners realize that the joys of running and improved fitness are not so much tied to performance as they are to the ability to remain active on a long-term basis, and that it is more important for running to fit into one's life as a form of healthful recreation than it is to take a few minutes off one's marathon time.

Of course, this does not mean that a lifetime of heavy training and competition cannot produce its own joyful rewards. It depends on how you go about it, and the spirit that governs your life in general and running in particular.

If there is one individual more than anyone who exemplifies the wonderful possibilities of the running experience, it is John A. Kelley, seventy-eight, of Massachusetts. A runner for sixty-three years, he was a member of four Olympic teams in the marathon, won the Boston

At a certain point, some runners seek the help of good coaching for running improvement. This happens to be Arthur Lydiard of New Zealand, one of the world's foremost coaching authorities. *(Tracy Frankel)*

Marathon twice, and in 1985 competed in the world-famous event for the fifty-fourth time. Kelley is a delightful, unassuming man. He can still run the marathon in under four hours, and seems to enjoy his running as much as ever.

In 1983, Kelley was given a complete physiological workup for the first time, to enable sports scientists to determine the effects of a lifetime of running on the health of a man Kelley's age. He was tested at the Aerobics Institute in Dallas, the world-famous facility developed by Dr. Kenneth Cooper, and the results showed Kelley to be in remarkable health. In fact he was said to be, at seventy-six, fitter than the average forty-year-old. This is a lesson for all of us.

Appendix I

A Sampling of
Leading American Road Races

Following are more than one hundred races of a variety of distances held annually throughout the United States. Be sure to request information about a given event in advance, and when doing so, always include a self-addressed stamped envelope.

JANUARY

MISSION BAY MARATHON, San Diego, CA. Contact: End of the Line, P.O. Box 1049, Coronado, CA 92118.

HOUSTON—TENNECO MARATHON, Houston, TX. Contact: Houston-Tenneco Marathon, P.O. Box 56682, Houston, TX 77027.

RUNNERS DEN/KOY CLASSIC, Phoenix, AZ. Contact: Valley Events, 8131 Buena Terra Way, Scottsdale, AZ 85253.

FREEZE YER GIZZARD BLIZZARD RUN 10K, International Falls, MN. Contact: Pat McKibbage, (218) 283-2345.

CHARLOTTE OBSERVER MARATHON, Charlotte, NC. Contact: Charlotte Observer Marathon, P.O. Box 30294, Charlotte, NC 28230.

ORANGE BOWL MARATHON, Miami, FL. Contact: Runners International, 10585 S. West Court, Suite 207, Miami, FL 33176.

WALT DISNEY WORLD/TRACK SHACK 10K, Lake Buena

Vista, FL. Contact: Track Shack, 1322 N. Mills Avenue, Orlando, FL 32803.

MANUFACTURERS HANOVER 5-MILER, New York,

NY. Contact: New York Road Runners Club, P.O. Box 881, FDR Station, New York, NY 10150.

SALISBURY 5-MILER, Salisbury, MA. Contact:

Fred Brown, 157 Walsh Street, Medford, MA 02155.

FEBRUARY

HAWAII WOMEN s 10K, Honolulu, HI. Contact: Honolulu Women Runners, P.O. Box 27487, Chinatown Sta., Honolulu, HI 96727.

SAMMAMISH VALLEY 10K, Bellevue, WA. Contact:

Eastside Track Club, c/o Bob Flexer, 14557 S.E. Fifty-first, Bellevue, WA 98006.

COWTOWN MARATHON, Fort Worth, TX. Contact:

Cowtown Marathon, P.O. Box 567, Fort Worth, TX 76101.

VALENTINE 5-MILE RACE, Loveland, CO. Contact:

Joe Friel, Fort Collins Track Club, c/o Foot of the Rockies, 1205 West Elizabeth, Fort Collins, CO 80521.

STATEHOOD DAY 1O-MILER, Lincoln, NE. Contact:

Roger Wiegand, 2400 Sheridan, Lincoln, NE 68502.

GASPARILLA DISTANCE CLASSIC 15K, Tampa, FL.

Contact: Gasparilla Distance Classic Assn., P.O. Box 1881, Tampa, FL 33601.

MARDI GRAS MARATHON, New Orleans, LA.

Contact: New Orleans Track Club, P.O. Box 30491, New Orleans, LA 70190.

BURGER KING HALF-MARATHON, Toccoa, GA. Contact: Tony Presley, Rte. 2, Defoor Road, Toccoa, GA 30577.

SNOWFLAKE 4-MILE RUN, New York, NY. Contact: New York Road Runners Club, P.O. Box 881, FDR Station, New York, NY 10150.

WINTER CARNIVAL 15K, Brattleboro, VT. Contact: Joseph Murphy, 140 Western Avenue, Brattleboro, VT 05301.

MARCH

OREGON RUNNER 10-MILER, Medford, OR. Contact: Oregon Runner, 2620F Barnett Road, Medford, OR 97501.

BONNE BELL 10K, San Diego, CA. Contact: San Diego Track Club, 1969 Gotham Street, Chula Vista, CA 92010.

CAPITOL 10,000-METER RUN, Austin, TX. Contact: Capitol 10,000, P.O. Box 670, Austin, TX 78767.

SEDALIA HALF-MARATHON, Sedalia, MO. Contact: Sedalia Runners Club, 500 W. Fifth Street, Sedalia, MO 65301.

VILAS HALF-MARATHON, Madison, WI. Contact: Bill Beecher, 206 Merryturn, Madison, WI 53714.

RIVER RUN 15K, Jacksonville, FL. Contact: River Run 15,000, 1545 University Boulevard West, Jacksonville, FL 32207.

COLONIAL HALF-MARATHON, Williamsburg, VA. Contact: Half-Marathon, P.O. Box 399, Williamsburg, VA 23187.

ATLANTA HALF-MARATHON, Atlanta, GA. Contact: Atlanta Track Club, 3097 E. Shadowlawn, Atlanta, GA 30305.

NIKE NEW JERSEY 10-MILER, Cherry Hill, NJ. Contact: George Hutchens, P.O. Box 3750, Cherry Hill, NJ 08034.

PERRIER CHERRY BLOSSOM 10-MILER, Washington, DC. Contact: Perrier Cherry Blossom, P.O. Box 4711, Arlington, VA 22204.

APRIL

BREAKERS YMCA 10-MILE RUN, Mission Beach, CA. Contact: End of the Line, P.O. Box 1049, Coronado, CA 92118.

KIWANIS 10K, Brinkley, AZ. Contact: Wayne Thompson, P.O. Box 38, Moro, AZ 72368.

CHERRY CREEK NORTH 5-MILER, Denver, CO. Contact: Rocky Mountain Road Runners, P.O. Box 17382, Denver, CO 80271.

GET IN GEAR 10K, Minneapolis, MN. Contact: Bill Kennedy, 2424 W. Twenty-fourth Street, Minneapolis, MN 55405.

CRYSTAL LAKE 5-MILER, Crystal Lake, IL. Contact: Crystal Lake Track Club, 88 Lincoln Parkway, Crystal Lake, IL 60014.

EASTER BEACH 4-MILER, Daytona Beach, FL. Contact: Daytona Beach Recreation Dept., P.O. Box 551, Daytona Beach, FL 32015.

RUN THROUGH HISTORY 10K, Beaufort, SC. Contact: Jack Cunningham, Star Route 5, Box 270A, Beaufort, SC 29002.

PERRIER 10K, New York, NY. Contact: New York Road Runners Club, P.O. Box 881, FDR Station, New York, NY 10150.

FREIHOFERS 10K RUN FOR WOMEN, Albany, NY. Contact: Freihofers Run, 382 Broadway, Albany, NY 12207.

BOSTON MILK RUN 10K, Boston, MA. Contact: John McGrath, P.O. Box 252, Boston, MA 02113.

BOSTON MARATHON, Hopkinton, MA. Contact: Boston Athletic Association, 17 Main Street, Hopkinton, MA 01748.

MAY

AVENUE OF THE GIANTS MARATHON, Weott, CA. Contact: Hal Jackson, P.O. Box 214, Arcata, CA 95521.

LILAC BLOOMSDAY RUN 12K, Spokane, WA. Contact: Don Kardong, P.O. Box 1511, Spokane, WA 99210.

BAY TO BREAKERS 12K, San Francisco, CA. Contact: Len Wallach, c/o San Francisco Examiner, 110 Fifth Street, San Francisco, CA 94103.

MILE HIGH MARATHON, Denver, CO. Contact: Rocky Mountain Road Runners, P.O. Box 17382, Denver, CO 80217.

BOLDER BOULDER 10K, Boulder, CO. Contact: Bank of Boulder, 3033 Iris Ave., Boulder, CO 80301.

SYTTENDE MAI 20-MILER, Madison, WI. Contact: Ed Hutchins, 134 E. Prospect, Stoughton, WI 53589.

REVCO MARATHON, Cleveland, OH. Contact: Reno Starnoni, P.O. Box 46604, Bedford, OH 44146.

COTTON Row RUN, 10K, Huntsville, AL. Contact: P.O. Box 292, Huntsville, AL 35804.

TREVIRA TWOSOME 10-MILER, New York, NY.

Contact: New York Road Runners Club, P.O. Box 881, FDR Station, New York, NY 10150.

YONKERS MARATHON, Yonkers, NY. Contact: Yonkers Marathon, P.O. Box 100, Yonkers, NY 10703.

JUNE

ALASKA WOMEN s 10K RUN, Anchorage, AK. Contact: Alaska Women's Run, 3605 Arctic AA, Anchorage, AK 99503.

CASCADE RUN OFF 15K, Portland, OR. Contact: Cascade Run Off, 208 S.W. Stark, Portland, OR 97204.

Go JUMP IN THE LAKE 10K, Okmulgee, OK. Contact: Okmulgee YMCA, 106 S. Kern, Okmulgee, OK 74447.

GARDEN OF THE GODS 10-MILER, Colorado Springs, CO. Contact: Dick Sutton, (303) 6851063.

SANTA FE RUN-AROUND 10K, Santa Fe, NM. Contact: Santa Fe Striders, P.O. Box 1818, Santa Fe, NM 87501.

JACKRABBIT 15K, Brookings, SD. Contact: South Dakota State University, Track Office, Brookings, SD 57007.

BELLIN 10K, Green Bay, WI. Contact: Bellin 10K, Bellin Memorial Hospital, P.O. Box 1700, Green Bay, WI 54305.

MICHIGAN CITY 15K, Michigan City, IN. Contact: Dunes Running Club, P.O. Box 42, Michigan City, IN 46360.

CITIZENS BANK 5-MILE CLASSIC, Morehead, KY. Contact: 5-Mile Classic, Rte. 6, Box 1302, Morehead, KY 40351.

HECHT'S 10-MILER, Washington, DC. Contact: Hecht's Public Relations, 7th and F streets, N.W., 7th Floor, Washington, DC 20004.

ORANGE CLASSIC 10K, Middletown, NY. Contact: Times Herald-Record, 40 Mulberry Street, Middletown, NY 10940.

JULY

CORONADO HALE-MARATHON, Coronado, CA. Contact: End of the Line, P.O. Box 1049, Coronado, CA 92118.

FOURTH OF JULY 6-MILER, Ashland, OR. Contact: Ashland Parks and Recreation, 59 Winburn Way, Ashland, OR 97520.

COPPER MOUNTAIN 5K and 10K, Copper Mountain, CO. Contact: Rocky Mountain Road Runners, P.O. Box 17382, Denver, CO 80217.

CHICAGO DISTANCE 20-K CLASSIC, Chicago, IL. Contact: Chicago Lung Assn., 1440 W. Washington Boulevard, Chicago, IL 60607.

BIX 7-MILER, Davenport, IA. Contact: Bix 7, P.O. Box 3828, Davenport, IA 52808.

FOURTH OF JULY 10K, Kingsport, TN. Contact: Kingsport Jaycees, Kingsport, TN 37664.

DODGER DASH, 5,000-meter Run, Vero Beach, FL. Contact: Vero Beach Dodgers, P.O. Box 2887, Vero Beach, FL 32960.

PEPSI CHALLENGE NATIONAL 10K CHAMPIONSHIPS, New York, NY. Contact: New York Road Runners Club, P.O. Box 881, FDR Station, New York, NY 10150.

L. L. BEAN 10K, Freeport, ME. Contact: Thad Dwyer, (207) 865-4761.

LAKELAND COUNTY FESTIVAL 10K, Greenville, PA. Contact: Ed McClimans, 183 College Avenue, Greenville, PA 16125.

PEACHTREE ROAD RACE 10K, Atlanta, GA. Contact: Atlanta Track Club, 3097 E. Shadowlawn Avenue, N.E., Atlanta, GA 30305.

AUGUST

FINEST CITY HALE-MARATHON, San Diego, CA. Contact: End of the Line, P.O. Box 1049, Coronado, CA 92118.

WORLD s HIGHEST 10K, Mammoth Lakes, CA. Contact: Mammoth Lakes Lions Club, P.O. Box 19, Mammoth Lakes, CA 93546.

PIKES PEAK MARATHON, Manitou Springs, CO. Contact: Pikes Peak Y, P.O. Box 1964, Colorado Springs, CO 80901.

WYOMING STATE FAIR 10K, Douglas, WY. Contact: Jericho Exploration, P.O. Box 1374, Douglas, WY 82633.

PAAVO NURMI MARATHON, Hurley, WI. Contact: Hurley Chamber of Commerce, 317 Silver Street, Hurley, WI 54534.

BOBBY CRIM 10-MILER, Flint, MI. Contact: Lois Craig, P.O. Box 481, Flint, MI 48501.

SUMMER BEACHES RUN 5-MILER, Jacksonville, FL. Contact: 416 S. Third Street, Jacksonville, FL 32250.

ASBURY PARK 10K CLASSIC, Asbury Park, NJ. Contact: Phil Benson, Box 2287, Ocean Township, NJ 07712.

FALMOUTH ROAD RACE 7-MILER, Falmouth, MA. Contact: Falmouth Road Race, P.O. Box 732, Falmouth, MA 02541.

FIRE FLY 7-MILER, Franklin, NY. Contact: Delaware County Runners, Box 251, Delhi, NY 13753.

SEPTEMBER

NIKE/OTC 25K, Eugene, OR. Contact: Nike Marathon, P.O. Box 10412, Eugene, OR 97440.

PREFONTAINE MEMORIAL 10K RUN, Coos Bay, OR. Contact: Pre Memorial Run, P.O. Box 210, Coos Bay, OR 97420.

KETCHUM 10-MILER, Ketchum, ID. Contact: P.O. Box 1844, Twin Falls, ID 83201.

AL McGUIRE 5-MILER, Milwaukee, WI. Contact: George Schansberg, (414) 224-2427.

CORRIDOR CLASSIC HALE-MARATHON, Dayton, OH. Contact: Stephen Barr, Miami Valley Hospital, 3700 Far Hills Avenue, Kettering, OH 45429.

CARTERS GROVE COUNTRY ROAD RACE 8-MILER, Newport News, VA. Contact: Dan Stebbins, 171 Winston Drive, Williamsburg, VA 23185.

FRANCONIA RAMBLE 10K, Franconia, NH. Contact: Franconia Ramble, c/o Bill Briggs, Franconia, NH 03580.

PHILADELPHIA DISTANCE RUN HALF-MARATHON, Philadelphia, PA. Contact: Philadelphia Distance Run, Central YMCA, 1421 Arch Street, Philadelphia, PA 19102.

OCTOBER

SACRAMENTO MARATHON, Sacramento, CA. Contact: John McIntosh, 4120 El Camino Avenue, Sacramento, CA 95821.

GOLDEN GATE MARATHON, San Francisco, CA. Contact: YMCA, (415) 392-4218.

RUN AGAINST CRIME 15K, El Paso, TX. Contact: Run Against Crime, 9040 Dwyer, El Paso, TX 79904.

GOVERNOR s CUP 10K, Denver, CO. Contact: Rocky Mountain Road Runners, P.O. Box 17382, Denver, CO 80217.

TWIN CITIES MARATHON, Minneapolis, MN. Contact: Jack Moran, (612) 373-2165.

BANK ONE MARATHON, Columbus, OH. Contact: Ohio Runner magazine, P.O. Box 2-215, Columbus, OH 43220.

HALLOWEEN 20K, Tuscaloosa, AL. Contact: Black Warrior Runners, P.O. Box 3067, Tuscaloosa, AL 35402.

EAST LYME MARATHON, East Lyme, CT. Contact: Bill Donovan, P.O. Box 26.2, East Lyme, CT 06333.

BONNE BELL WOMEN s NATIONAL 10K CHAMPIONSHIP, Boston, MA. Contact: Conventures, 45

Newbury Street, Boston, MA 02116.

NOVEMBER

NEW YORK CITY MARATHON, New York, NY. Contact: New York Road Runners Club, P.O. Box 881, FDR Station, New York, NY 10150.

RIVERSIDE 10-MILER, Tulsa, OK. Contact: Joe McDaniel, P.O. Box 3305, Tulsa, OK 74101.

RUN FOR THE BIRDS 5-MILER, Rochester, MI. Contact: Dave Kanners, Oakland Runners Club, Box 731, Rochester, MI 48063.

WENDY 10K CLASSIC, Bowling Green, KY. Contact: David Mason, P.O. Box 1316, Bowling Green, KY 42101.

HEALTH RUN 10K, Biloxi, MS. Contact: Gulf Coast Running Club, P.O. Box 4921 WBS, Biloxi, MS 39531.

ARKANSAS 20K, Benton, AR. Contact: Ray Love, 312 Pope Drive, Benton, AR 72015.

MARINE CORPS MARATHON, Washington, DC. Contact: Marine Corps Marathon, P.O. Box 188, Quantico, VA 22134.

BERWICK RUN FOR THE DIAMONDS 9-MILER, Berwick, PA. Contact: Berwick Marathon Assn., P.O. Box 856, Berwick, PA 18603.

DECEMBER

HONOLULU MARATHON, Honolulu, HI. Contact: P.O. Box 27244, Chinatown Station, Honolulu, HI 96827.

FIESTA BOWL MARATHON, Scottsdale, AZ. Contact: Scottsdale Charros, P.O. Box 1032, Scottsdale, AZ 85252.

ROCKET CITY MARATHON, Huntsville, AL. Contact: Harold Tinsley, 8811 Edgehill Drive, Huntsville, AL 35802.

BRIAN'S RUN 10K, West Chester, PA. Contact: Larry Brandon, 206 Brooke Drive, West Chester, PA 19380.

SANTA'S 3.5-MILE RUN, Glastonbury, CT. Contact: Santa's Run, 2155 Main Street, Glastonbury, CT 06033.

RUNNER'S WORLD MAGAZINE NEW YEAR'S EVE 5-MILER. Contact: New York Road Runners Club, P.O. Box 881, FDR Station, New York, NY 10150.

Appendix II

For Further Reading

Here is a sampling of books on running and fitness that can serve as an additional source of information. Most of the books are fairly current, though some were published several years ago.

TRAINING

Bloom, Marc. *Cross Country Running*. Mountain View, CA: World Publications, 1978.

Costill, Dr. David L. A *Scientific Approach to Distance Running*. Los Altos, CA: *Track & Field News*, 1979.

Dunaway, James O.; and the editors of *Sports Illustrated*. *Track: Running Events*. Philadelphia: Lippincott, 1972.

Fixx, James F. *The Complete Book of Running*. New York: Random House, 1977.

_____.. *Jim Fixx's Second Book of Running*. New York: Random House, 1980.

Galloway, *Jeff*. *Galloway's Book on Running*. Atlanta: Galloway, 1983.

Glover, Bob; and Jack Shepherd. *The Runner's Handbook*. New York: Penguin, 1978.

Glover, Bob; and Pete Schuder. *The Competitive Runner's Handbook*. New York: Penguin, 1983.

Henderson, Joe. *Running A to Z: An Encyclopedia for the Thoughtful Runner*. Brattleboro, VT: Stephen Greene, 1983.

_____.. *Run Farther, Run Faster*. Mountain View, CA: World Publications, 1979.

Squires, Bill; with Raymond Krise. *Improving Your Running*. Brattleboro, VT: Stephen Greene, 1982.

Wilt, Fred. *Run, Run, Run.* Los Altos, CA: *Track Field News,* 1964.

THE MARATHON

Bloom, Marc. *The Marathon: What It Takes to Go the Distance.* New
York: Holt, Rinehart & Winston, 1981.

Brown, Skip; and John Graham. *Target 26.* New York: Collier, 1979.

Friedberg, Ardy. *How to Run Your First Marathon.* New York: Simon
& Schuster, 1982.

Martin, David; and Roger Gynn. *The Marathon Footrace.* Springfield,
IL: Thomas, 1979.

Shapiro, James E. *On the Road: The Marathon.* New York:
Crown, 1978.

INJURY

Mangi, Richard; with Peter Jokl and O. William Dayton. *The Runner's
Complete Medical Guide.* New York: Summit, 1979.

McGregor, Dr. Rob Roy; and Stephen E. Devereux. EEVeTeC; *The
McGregor Solution for Managing the Pains of Fitness.* Boston:
Houghton Mifflin, 1982.

Mirkin, Dr. Gabe; and Marshall Hoffman. *The Sportsmedicine Book.*
Boston: Little, Brown, 1978.

Southmayd, Dr. William; and Marshall Hoffman. *Sports Health.* New
York: Quick Fox, 1981.

Weisenfeld, Dr. Murray F.; with Barbara Burr. *Runner's Repair Manu-
al.* New York: St. Martin's Press, 1980.

Wood, Dr. Peter. *Run to Health.* New York: Grosset & Dunlap, 1980.

NUTRITION

Bayrd, Ned; and Chris Quilter. *Food for Champions.* Boston:
Houghton Mifflin, 1982.

Bronfen, Nan. *Nutrition for a Better Life.* Santa Barbara, CA:
Capra, 1980.

Clark, Nancy. *The Athlete's Kitchen.* New York: Bantam, 1980.

Darden, Ellington. *Nutrition and Athletic Performance.* Pasadena, CA:
Athletic Press, 1976.

Haas, Dr. Robert. *Eat to Win.* New York: Rawson, 1983.

Katch, Frank I.; and William D. McArdle. *Nutrition, Weight Control and Exercise.* Boston: Houghton Mifflin, 1977.

Morella, Joseph J., and Richard J. Turchetti. *Nutrition and the Athlete,* New York: Van Nostrand Reinhold, 1982.

WEIGHT TRAINING

Darden, Ellington. *The Nautilus Book.* Chicago: Contemporary Books, 1982.

Friedberg, Ardy. *Weight Training for Runners.* New York: Simon & Schuster, 1981.

Peterson, James A. *Total Fitness: The Nautilus Way.* New York: Leisure Press, 1978.

Schwartz, Dr. Leonard. *Heavyhands: The Ultimate Exercise.* Boston: Little, Brown, 1982.

GENERAL FITNESS

Cooper, Dr. Kenneth H. *Aerobics.* New York: Evans, 1968.

_____.. *The New Aerobics.* New York: Evans, 1970.

_____.. *The Aerobics Program for Total Well-Being.* New York: Bantam, 1983.

_____.. *Running Without Fear.* New York: Evans, 1985.

Getchell, Bud; with Wayne Anderson. *Being Fit.* New York: Wiley, 1982.

Higdon, Hal. *Fitness After Forty.* Mountain View, CA: World Publications, 1977.

Jerome, John. *Staying with It.* New York: Viking, 1984.

Kostrubala, Dr. Thaddeus. *The Joy of Running.* Philadelphia: Lippincott, 1976.

Maule, Tex. *Running for Life.* London: Pelham, 1973.

Perry, Paul. *Paul Perry's Complete Book of the Triathlon.* New York: New American Library, 1983.

Sachs, Dr. Michael H.; and Michael L. Sachs. *Psychology of Running.* Champaign, IL: Human Kinetics, 1981.

Shapiro, James E. *Meditations from the Breakdown Lane.* New York: Random House, 1982.

Sheehan, Dr. George. *Running and Being.* New York: Simon & Schuster, 1978.

_____.. *This Running Life.* New York: Simon & Schuster, 1980.

_____.. *How to Feel Great 24 Hours a Day.* New York: Simon & Schuster, 1983.

Ullyot, Dr. Joan. *Running Free.* New York: Perigee, 1980.

Wilmore, Dr. Jack H. *The Wilmore Fitness Program.* New York: Simon & Schuster/Wallaby, 1981.

BIOGRAPHY AND AUTOBIOGRAPHY

Bannister, Roger. *The Four-Minute Mile.* New York: Dodd, Mead, 1955, rev. ed. 1981.

Berry, Theodore J.; and James Francis "Jumbo" Elliott. *Jumbo Elliott: Maker of Milers, Maker of Men.* New York: St. Martin's Press, 1982.

Chodes, John. *Corbitt.* Los Altos, CA: Tafnews, 1974.

Coe, Sebastian; with David Miller. *Running Free.* New York: St. Martin's Press, 1981.

Jordan, Tom. *Pre!* Los Altos, CA: Tafnews, 1977.

Liquori, Marty; and Skip Myslenski. *On the Run.* New York: Morrow, 1979.

Moore, Kenny. *Best Efforts.* Garden City, N.Y.: Doubleday, 1982.

Rodgers, Bill; with Joe Concannon. *One for the Road.* New York: Simon & Schuster, 1980.

Shorter, Frank; with Marc Bloom. Olympic Gold: *A Runner's Life and Times.* Boston, MA: Houghton Mifflin, 1984.

About the Author

Marc Bloom, a senior writer for *Runner's World* and track-and-field features writer for the New York *Times,* has been writing on health, fitness, and running for twenty-five years. His articles have appeared in leading magazines nationwide. In addition to Olympic Gold, which he wrote with Frank Shorter, he is the author of *Cross-Country Running* and *The Marathon.* Bloom is the 1983 recipient of the Road Runners Club of America's Journalism Award.